A COMPASS
TO
FULFILLMENT

A COMPASS TO FULFILLMENT

*Passion and Spirituality
in Life and Business*

KAZUO INAMORI

New York   Chicago   San Francisco
Lisbon   London   Madrid   Mexico City   Milan
New Delhi   San Juan   Seoul   Singapore
Sydney   Toronto

Ikikata by Kazuo Inamori. Copyright © 2004 by Kazuo Inamori.
Copyright for English translation © 2009 by Cathy Hirano.
Original Japanese edition published by Sunmark Publishing, Inc., Tokyo, Japan.
English translation rights arranged with Sunmark Publishing, Inc., through InterRights, Inc., Tokyo.

1 2 3 4 5 6 7 8 9 0   DOC/DOC   0 1 0 9

ISBN: 978-0-07-161509-9
MHID: 0-07-161509-1

McGraw-Hill books are available at special quantity discounts to use as premiums and sales promotions, or for use in corporate training programs. To contact a representative please visit the Contact Us pages at www.mhprofessional.com.

Library of Congress Cataloging-in-Publication Data

Inamori, Kazuo.
    [Ikikata. English]
    A compass to fulfillment : passion and spirituality in life and business / by Kazuo Inamori.
        p. cm.
    ISBN 978-0-07-161509-9 (alk. paper)
    1. Success. 2. Conduct of life. 3. Success in business. 4. Self-realization. I. Title.
    BF637.S8.I5313 2009
    650.1--dc22
                                                                        2009026358

CONTENTS

INTRODUCTION

I am delighted that *A Compass to Fulfillment* is being published in English. This book is an exploration of the way people should think and live as human beings. I sincerely hope that the philosophy expressed here will transcend the barriers of ethnicity, language, culture, and religion and communicate on a universal level.

Since its publication in 2004, the Japanese edition of *A Compass to Fulfillment* has become a bestseller in Japan, with over 600,000 copies sold. It also has been published in China, Taiwan, and Korea, as well as in Russia and Lithuania, and the book is being translated into Spanish and Portuguese. The letters sent to me by people from other countries expressing their support for my philosophy are a clear indication that the perspective presented in this book is relevant to other cultures, not just to Japan.

I am very fortunate to have been able to establish two companies, Kyocera and KDDI, both of which are listed in the

Fortune 500. During the seven decades of my life, I have become strongly convinced that the human mind cannot only change the life of the individual, but it also can have a broad and significant impact on society.

I believe that the issues currently confronting the human race, including environmental destruction, terrorism, and international disputes, are caused by evil thoughts that each individual harbors in his or her mind. When I say "evil thoughts," I am referring to the selfish, unbounded greed that has been the driving force behind the worrisome trajectory of our current civilization.

Modern civilization developed rapidly after the onset of the Industrial Revolution about 250 years ago. Although it arose partially from human curiosity and the search for truth, it also was propelled by insatiable greed and egotism: the human desire to be richer. Driven by the engine of greed, humankind mastered wisdom, advanced scientific technology, and developed the economy. Now, however, we are facing the consequences of our desire for excess: environmental destruction, depleted energy resources, terrorism, and conflict.

Despite the fallout of our actions, people continue to seek even greater wealth and spend their lives desperately trying to fulfill their every desire. Can we go on like this? I believe that we can't. If the human race is to survive, we must change the human mind, the driving force of civilization, and adopt a different attitude as the standard for our way of living.

The financial crisis sparked by the collapse of subprime loans in the United States in 2008 is sweeping across the world. Financial markets are in a state of chaos, and that is beginning to have a serious impact on economies worldwide. Although the immediate cause was excessive mismanagement of financial derivative products, the root cause was the headlong push of capitalism to maximize profit and satisfy people's greed. In that sense, the current financial crisis can be viewed as a divine warning to the human race.

It is time that we explore how to base our way of life not on economic growth driven by selfish desire, but on consideration, love, affection, and altruism. It is my ardent hope that this book, which is based on this philosophy, will reach the hearts of many English-language readers and help them live more fruitful lives and contribute to a better world.

From Kyoto, the ancient capital of Japan, on an April day in 2009, in a blizzard of cherry petals.

KAZUO INAMORI
Founder and Chairman Emeritus, Kyocera

PROLOGUE

Reexamining the Meaning of Life in an Age of Chaos

We live in an age of anxiety and deepening confusion, which has made us unable to see our way forward. Although affluent, we feel unfulfilled; although blessed with material necessities, we lack civility; although ostensibly free, we feel somehow confined. If we have the will and make the effort, anything is possible and everything is within our grasp; yet, we feel powerless and pessimistic, and some of us may even sink into crime or immorality.

How did we reach this impasse? Could it be because so many people fail to find meaning in their lives or the value in living, because we have lost the inner compass that guides us through life? I believe that the answer is yes and that the current confusion in society stems from the lack of a constructive philosophy for living. In this day, the first and most important step we can take is to confront that fundamental question—what is the purpose of life?—and in doing so attempt to develop a philosophy, a system of beliefs, or a set of principles that will serve as a guideline for living.

Pondering our purpose in life may seem as futile as digging for water in the desert or as difficult as trying to dam a rushing river, yet this simple, straightforward exercise is even more relevant in light of society's tendency to belittle earnest effort. If we avoid thinking deeply about the purpose of our lives as chaos continues to spread throughout society, our confusion will increase and our future will become more uncertain. I believe that many people feel, as I do, a great urgency about this situation.

In this book I would like not only to examine what it means to be human but to explore the purpose of life and how to live it as well. It is my hope that the philosophy I present in these pages will drive at least a modest stake into the rushing stream of the times. It will be deeply satisfying for me if my words help you take joy in living and lead you to a happy, fulfilling life.

The Meaning of Life Is in Refining the Soul

What, then, is the meaning or purpose of life? I believe that it is nothing less than to elevate our minds and refine our souls.

It is human nature to be blinded and led astray by selfish desires. Left to our own devices, we would yearn ceaselessly for wealth, status, and fame and drown ourselves in hedonistic pleasures. Of course, we need to make enough money to lead a comfortable life, and we cannot unconditionally condemn the desire to succeed, as it is what motivates us to persevere in life.

However, all these things are limited to this temporal world. No matter how much we accumulate, we cannot take any of it with us when we die. In the end, we must settle our accounts here. The only thing that does not perish is the soul. It is all we can take with us on the new journey that begins when death makes us shed the status, fame, and wealth that we acquired in this world.

If you asked me, "What did you come here to accomplish?" I would reply unhesitatingly that I came to become a better person than I was at birth, that I came to die with a soul that is nobler and purer than the one I was born into, no matter how slight the improvement. To me, this is the only purpose in life: to live fully in the temporal plane, savoring all its joys and sorrows, washed by the waves of good fortune and bad, and to use my time on earth as a fine sand that refines my nature as a human being and cultivates my spirit so that I leave this world with my soul in a higher state. It is in this persistent striving to make each day better than the one before, this simple search for truth, that the purpose and value of life can be found.

Granted, there seems to be more pain than pleasure in living. At times we may wonder why we have to suffer so much, and we may come to resent God or the Buddha, but it is precisely because we live in a world of suffering that we can benefit from viewing pain as a test that develops the soul. Suffering is actually the ultimate opportunity to hone our true nature. People who can see tests as opportunities are able to make their limited time on earth their own. Life is the time given to us to refine our minds and to cultivate our souls, and it is in the process of living that we will find meaning and value in our lives.

Simple Principles Make Unshakable Guidelines

Our approach to life directly affects us, burnishing or tarnishing our souls, ennobling or degrading our minds. Many talented people lose their way in life because their moral standards are not on par with their ability. This is especially true in the business world. Many people commit dishonest acts in the pursuit of personal profit. They may have a flair for business, but their behavior is puzzling. Perhaps it is because they are so talented that they become overconfident and take themselves down the wrong path. In utilizing their talent, they may initially succeed, but once they start relying upon their own cleverness alone, they begin heading toward failure.

The more extraordinary your ability, the more you will need a compass to guide you in the right direction. Think of that guiding compass as your philosophy. If you lack a philosophy and your character is not mature, if you have talent but no virtue, you will be unable to steer yourself in the right direction, no matter how skilled you may be. This is true for everyone, not just for business leaders.

I think of character as a simple formula: personality + philosophy = character. Our character, which represents the nobility of our soul, consists of the personality we were born with and the philosophy that we acquire as we undergo life's lessons. Therefore, the philosophy on which we base our way of life determines our character. If it is not deep-rooted, the tree of our character cannot grow straight and sturdy. We need to live by those simple, basic principles that teach us right from wrong, that have been passed down from one generation to the next and constitute the ethics and moral standards cultivated by humankind since ancient times.

I started Kyocera Corporation when I was 27 years old with help from many others, but I had very little experience in management and only a vague idea of how to run a business successfully. At a loss as to how to proceed, I decided that I would be true to what I felt was right as a human being. Don't lie; never harm anyone; don't be greedy or selfish—I took these simple precepts that we learn from our parents and teachers but tend to forget as we grow older and applied them directly to business policy, adopting them as my decision-making criteria. Although I knew little about business practices, I was convinced that success cannot be gained by defying generally accepted moral values.

It was a very simple standard, but for that reason it made sense, and I was able to keep our company on the right track, with excellent results. If you are looking for the key to my success, this is undoubtedly it: Although I lacked talent, I followed the simple yet powerful principle of pursuing what is right as a human being. This is the most important guideline in my life, and I constantly remind myself of it by asking myself: Is this choice compatible with what it means to be human? Does this decision conform to the most basic ethical and moral principles?

To many people in Japan today, the idea of ethics or morals as guidelines for living sounds outdated. During World War II, moral education in Japan was misused to manipulate people, and today, in reaction, its very mention is taboo. Yet these moral values were originally the fruit of a wisdom cultivated by humankind and the standard that guided daily life. People in modern Japan have discarded much of the wisdom of past generations, claiming it is outmoded, and in their pursuit of convenience they have lost much that was essential, including ethics and morals.

I believe that we are being called upon to return to those fundamental principles and live our lives in accordance with them. I believe it is time to retrieve this precious knowledge.

Mastering the Truth of Life through Hard Work

How, then, can we build character and refine our souls? Do we need to undertake some special practice, such as retreating into the mountains or standing under a waterfall? The answer is no. On the contrary, striving daily to do one's best in this material world is the key.

As will be discussed later in this book, the Buddha taught the importance of *shojin*, or making a diligent effort, as a practice through which people can begin to attain a state of enlightenment. To do your very best, to focus fully on the task before you without allowing yourself to become distracted—this is *shojin*. The prevailing view, however, is that work is only a means to make a living, that it is even a necessary evil, and the ideal is to work as little as possible for as much money as possible so that you can spend the rest of your time pursuing other interests or pleasures. Accomplishing this, to some, is at the heart of living a prosperous lifestyle.

However, the act of working has far more significance and value to us as human beings than just providing a livelihood. It can help us rise above our selfish desires and is the most effective way to develop our minds and build our characters. Putting our heart and soul into the task before us is an extremely important, noble practice that makes us better human beings.

Take, for example, Ninomiya Sontoku (1787–1856), an uneducated peasant who was born and raised in poverty. Every day he went out before dawn and worked the fields diligently until dark with only a hoe and a plow. Through hard work alone, he transformed many impoverished rural villages into prosperous communities. In recognition of that outstanding feat, he was recruited by the Tokugawa government and invited to the palace, where he mixed with members of the upper class. Despite the fact that he had not been trained in social niceties, he bore himself with the dignity of a true nobleman and emanated spirituality. Those long days toiling in the fields, covered in dirt and sweat, had nurtured his inner being, cultivated his character, purified his heart, and honed his soul, raising him to a higher plane of existence.

Many people imagine that refining one's soul must involve some form of religious practice when in fact all you need to do is love your work and give it your best effort. People who put their best into what they do will find that their efforts bring about the natural evolution of their souls and the strengthening of their character. This is the nobility of the act of working.

I believe there is a Latin saying that instead of perfecting the work, we should perfect the person who performs it. In fact, however, it is through hard work that a person can perfect her character. Philosophy is borne of hard-earned sweat, and the heart is trained through daily endeavor. Immersing yourself in the task that needs doing, being innovative in your approach, and making consistent efforts lead to an appreciation of this particular day, this particular moment, that has been given to you.

I often advise my employees, "Live each day with complete sincerity." By this I mean sincerity so complete that we do not waste one moment of our precious lives. Living with this simple honesty will transform even the most ordinary person into an extraordinary one. This is the path followed by the people we regard as masters in any particular field. Work not only generates economic value but also increases our worth as human beings. Thus, there is no need to withdraw from the temporal world. The workplace is the perfect field for cultivating the spirit, and working is a spiritual practice. By giving our best to our work every day, we not only develop a noble character but also can gain true happiness in life.

Change Your Thinking and Transform Your Life

What do we need to live a better life and obtain the fruit called happiness? For me, the answer is found in the following formula:

$$\text{The result of work and life} = \text{attitude} \times \text{effort} \times \text{ability}$$

Let me emphasize that the results of our work and our lives are derived not from the addition but from the multiplication of these three factors.

Ability refers to our talents and intellect, which are generally inherent traits. Health and good reflexes also fall into this category. In contrast, effort, which is the extent to which we are passionately involved in what we do and dedicated to our work and lives, is an acquired trait that we can control. I rate both ability and effort on a scale from zero to 100. Because these factors are multiplied rather than added, a person with great ability who exerts very little effort will produce poor results. However, a person who lacks ability but lives and works passionately can produce greater results because people like that recognize their inadequacy and work hard to overcome it.

Of the three elements in the formula, however, attitude is the most important factor, the one that determines our lives. By attitude I mean your state of mind and your approach to living. This includes your personal philosophy or beliefs. This is the only factor that I have ranked from −100 to +100. Therefore, according to the terms of the formula, even if you have ability and make diligent efforts, if your attitude is negative, you will encounter negative results.

Let me share an embarrassing example from my past. I graduated from university during an economic downturn, and there were few jobs available for new graduates. Lacking influential connections, I was rejected for every position for which I applied. At one point, frustrated and disillusioned with the workforce and the way it takes advantage of the weak, I toyed with the idea of joining the Japanese underworld. Although its members' activities were criminal, their world seemed at least to be governed by principles of duty and loyalty. If I had chosen the path of an educated gangster, however, I never would have been happy or fulfilled, even if I had become a gang leader, because the underlying philosophy is warped and negative.

What, then, is a positive attitude? I think the answer is quite simple: "right-mindedness," which is based on common sense. It involves maintaining optimism, a constructive attitude, gratitude, cheerfulness, cooperativeness, goodwill, consideration, kindness, diligence, contentment, selflessness, and detachment. These qualities may sound very ordinary—a list of moral principles we learn in elementary school—but that is no reason to consider them with contempt. Rather than understanding such virtues intellectually, we need to internalize them and make them our own.

What We Think Becomes Reality: The Law of the Universe

To maintain right-mindedness, to passionately develop our inherent abilities, is the secret to success in life because it is in conformity with the law of the universe. There is a Buddhist teaching that advises that thoughts create karma, which generates all experience. In other words, our thoughts generate impulses that become reality. Therefore, the way we think is extremely important and should be kept free from negativity. For that reason, Tempu Nakamura (1876–1968), a philosopher and proponent of positive thinking, said that we should never paint a negative image in our minds. Strong thoughts manifest as real experience, and the mental images we create shape our lives. It is important to keep this law in mind.

Some may dismiss this concept as fantasy, but I assure you that it is an absolute law that I have verified through personal experience. People who think positive thoughts lead good lives. Conversely, life does not go well for those who harbor negativity in their minds. Although we may not realize it at first because it takes time for the results of our actions to become apparent, in the long run people's lives generally turn out the way they pictured them. We need a pure heart when thinking about our way of life because good thoughts, particularly thoughts that are focused on service to others, are in alignment with the original intent of the universe.

There is a cosmic force that seeks to cultivate all things, that encourages development and evolution. I call this the will of the universe. If we can align ourselves with it, we will find true success and prosperity. Similarly, if we turn away from it, we will stop progressing and eventually decline. If our approach to life is altruistic, our thoughts focused on the good of all, our hearts filled with love, and our efforts consistent, this force will buoy us and our lives will be fulfilling. In contrast, if our hearts and minds are occupied with envy, hatred, and selfish desires, our lives will deteriorate rapidly.

The will that suffuses the universe overflows with love, sincerity, and harmony. It acts on all things equally and seeks to guide all creation in a positive direction toward growth and development. The Big Bang theory, which I discuss in more detail in Chapter 5, is a convincing example of this. According to this concept, the universe began with only a small handful of elementary particles. Those particles were united through a massive explosion, creating the protons, neutrons, and mesons that make up atomic nuclei. The atomic nuclei joined with electrons to produce hydrogen, the first type of atom. Various other types of atoms formed, followed by molecules and macromolecules, and then by higher organisms, such as human beings. The more I learn about the evolutionary process in the universe, the more I am convinced of the intervention of a greater will that promotes growth and progress.

During my many years of involvement in the creative process of product development, I have sensed the existence of "Something Great" many times. In fact, my success in product development was achieved through tapping into this greater wisdom and allowing it to lead me.

Kyocera is a leading producer of fine ceramics, a general-purpose advanced material used in high-tech products, such as computers and cell phones, and we pride ourselves on consistently opening up new horizons in this field. When I entered the workforce, however, I knew nothing about ceramics. The only job I could find after graduating happened to be with a company in Kyoto that specialized in porcelain insulators. My job required knowledge of inorganic chemistry, but in university I had majored in organic chemistry, such as petrochemistry. Not only did I lack the basic knowledge and skills needed for the job, but the company, which had a chronic deficit, could provide only the most rudimentary research equipment and facilities. I had no choice but to find ways to conduct research and experimental development with the tools at hand. Despite those handicaps, I succeeded in producing Japan's first synthetic fine ceramic material in a very little time.

Only a year earlier, General Electric had produced an identical material. My methodology, however, was completely original and did not involve consecutive experiments using precision equipment. It seemed like sheer luck that an unknown researcher working for a tiny insulator manufacturer in Kyoto could have produced results that rivaled those of one of the world's top manufacturers. However, my luck persisted even after I quit the company and established Kyocera, and it is what helped both my new enterprise and me grow.

An Inexhaustible Treasury of Wisdom

I am sure that this continued good fortune was not the result of any talent I possessed, and neither was it a coincidence. Rather, I think that somewhere in the universe there is a treasury of wisdom. We draw on the wisdom stored there, and it comes to us in the form of a new idea, an inspiration, or creativity. It is like a well of knowledge, of universal truth, belonging to God or the universe, not to any human being. Technology advances and civilization develops through what we receive from this store.

As is explained later in this book, I established the Kyoto Prize to support people in many fields who are opening up new horizons for humankind. Amazingly, all of the award recipients say that their discoveries came through a sudden inspiration that seemed like a revelation from God. That instant of creation may come in the middle of intense research, during a break, or even in a dream. I think it is likely that the inspiration for Edison's many groundbreaking inventions in the field of telecommunications came from that treasury of wisdom in response to his tremendous efforts. Whenever I look at the achievements of the masters who have gone before us, I am convinced that this treasury is the source of new knowledge and technological inventions; this is how creative production and civilization progress.

How can we open the door to access that wisdom? I think the only answer is to be passionate about what you are doing and strive sincerely to do your best. When you strive toward a goal with good intentions and earnest effort, I believe that God illuminates the way with a ray of light from the treasury of wisdom. How else could someone like me, without knowledge or skills and with very little experience or equipment, have broken new ground at the international level? At that time, I threw myself into the research with maniacal passion, driven by an ardent desire to see my research bear fruit. I approached the task single-mindedly, and in return, I believe that I was given a drop of wisdom from that treasury.

Exercise Constant Self-Discipline to Follow the Kingly Way

Some may call this treasury Providence or the wisdom of the Creator, but whatever its name, it is ceaselessly urging humankind toward growth and development. It concerns me, however, to see many people using the wisdom from that treasury in the wrong way or for the wrong purpose, and I worry that the human race has lost sight of where it should be heading. I believe this situation reflects the loss of a philosophy for living. Although we have established a highly advanced civilization that is based on scientific technology, although we enjoy great affluence, we have forgotten the importance of our spiritual and moral nature. This has generated new problems, such as environmental destruction.

Thanks to scientific advancements, we can perform "miracles" and wield new powers freely. We have taken advanced technology and knowledge, which was formerly the domain of God, as our own and have begun to use it as we please. However, the consequences have been negative. The environment of the planet and therefore our very existence are being threatened by the destruction of the ozone layer, by agrochemicals in the soil and water, by increasing carbon emissions and the resultant global warming, and by the effects of environmental hormones, such as dioxins. These are all examples of how we have used the knowledge intended for our happiness in the wrong way. We are destroying ourselves with weapons that we have created.

As my formula for life demonstrates, no matter how advanced our technology or knowledge (ability) is and no matter how diligent we are in our efforts, if we do not develop the right attitude, the philosophy, beliefs, or ideology that will guide us through life, in the end we will inflict tremendous suffering on this planet. Thus, the issue of how we should live our lives as human beings is far more than a personal issue. Each of us needs to reexamine his or her way of life if we are to save the world and move humankind in the right direction.

To do this, a highly disciplined approach to life that embraces hard work and self-control is essential. Diligence, sincerity, earnestness, honesty—we must make basic moral standards and ethical principles like these the solid foundation for our philosophy, for our way of life. In this age, we are being called upon to aspire to and follow the way of life that is right for us as human beings. In the language of the ancients this was called the kingly way, and it leads to success and prosperity, to peace and happiness, for the entire human race. I hope that this book will serve as a manual for this way of life.

A COMPASS
TO
FULFILLMENT

CHAPTER 1

MAKING OUR DESIRES REALITY

You Only Get What You Ask For

"Life never goes the way I want." It is easy to take such a narrow view of the events that happen in our lives. This outlook, however, is self-fulfilling. It is precisely because we expect that life will not work out according to our wishes that life doesn't go the way we want it to. In this sense, our lives fulfill our expectations.

Many philosophies for success are rooted in the view that life is an expression of the mind. On the basis of personal experience, I am a firm believer in this idea. We attract only the outcomes on which we focus; only those things we strongly desire are within the realm of our realization. It is impossible to draw a specific result toward us without holding it firmly in our minds. Thus, our state of mind and that which we desire shape the reality of our lives. If you want to achieve a particular outcome, the first step is to focus your mind on the image of who you want to become or the situation that you want to come to pass. You must hold that thought with greater determination than anyone else and desire it with passionate intensity.

I first became aware of the power of the mind over 40 years ago at a lecture by Konosuke Matsushita (1894–1989), who was regarded by many Japanese people as the "god of management." At the time of the lecture, Matsushita had not yet been idolized to the extent that he is now, and I had only just started my company, which was still a small, unknown firm. During his lecture, Matsushita spoke about his famous "dam management" theory, whose concepts are as follows. A river without a dam floods during heavy rain and dries to a trickle during droughts. However, if we dam the river and store its water, we can gain control over the river so that we are no longer at the mercy of the weather or the environment. The same principle, he claimed, can be applied to management. He recommended that companies create reserves, such as equipment reserves and capital reserves, during times of plenty to ensure stable growth in times of scarcity.

Sitting in the back of the room, I could almost see a wave of dissent spread across the audience of the managers of small and medium-size businesses like myself. "What's he talking about?" people muttered. "We *can't* do that. That's why we have to struggle night and day. If we had enough leeway to do that, things wouldn't be such a struggle. We already know we need a reserve. What we don't know is how to make one."

During the question and answer period at the end of Matsushita's talk, a man stood up and voiced his frustration: "Obviously dam-style management would be ideal if it were possible. But it's not. If you aren't going to tell us how to build a dam, what's the point?"

A wry smile crossed Matsushita's gentle face. He sat silently, thinking for several moments, and then said simply, "To be honest, I don't know how either. I don't know how, but I still have to want to make one." He did not seem to have answered the question, and the audience laughed uncomfortably. Although most of the people were clearly disappointed, I sat stunned, electrified by his words. He had revealed a profound truth.

Whether Sleeping or Awake, Stay Passionately Focused

Matsushita's remark made me realize how important it is to desire something. It made no sense for him to try to teach us how to make a dam, because each person, regardless of Matsushita's instructions, would have approached the construction process in his or her own way. First we had to *want* to make one. That desire is the beginning of everything.

Until the heart cries out with longing, we cannot see our goal or how to achieve it, and success comes no closer. This is why it is so important to have a constant and ardent desire. This yearning is the starting point, the one thing that is guaranteed to make our dreams come true. Life is an expression of our minds, and our desires are the original and vital force through which our dreams are realized. Like seeds planted in the garden of life, our desires sink roots, raise their branches to the sky, blossom, and bear fruit. It was this truth—a truth that penetrates our lives even though we catch only occasional glimpses of it—that I gleaned from Matsushita's words. Subsequently, I experienced and gradually mastered this truth in my own life.

A vague, halfhearted desire will never lead to results. You must have a tremendous longing, a fierce yearning that occupies your thoughts from night to day, no matter if you are sleeping or awake. It must fill your being from head to toe so that if you cut yourself with a knife, it would not be blood but longing that seeped from your skin. The driving force behind all accomplishments is this kind of single-minded intense desire.

If one person fails where another succeeds despite having the same ability and exerting the same amount of effort, people often assume that the difference is due to luck. In fact, however, it is due to the size, depth, and intensity of each person's desire. Some may consider me naively optimistic, but remember, it is far from easy to focus your thoughts so intently on a single purpose that you forget to eat and sleep, and it is no simple feat to maintain this passionate desire until it penetrates your subconscious mind.

In business management and in new venture development, common sense often tells us that something new or different is doomed to failure. If we let common sense dictate our actions, however, the possible will become impossible. If you sincerely wish to start something new, the first requisite is to passionately focus your mind and heart on it. To make the impossible possible you must be "crazy" about the idea and work toward it with the positive conviction that you can accomplish anything. This is the only way to achieve your goals in life and in business.

Visualize the Realization of Your Goals in Living Color

The claim that passionate desire is the mother of success sounds so unscientific that some people may dismiss it as a kind of mentalism. Experience, however, has taught me that if I am thinking about an idea constantly, I will be able to visualize the outcome very clearly.

All successes in life start with a strong desire to do something. I pursue an idea, thinking intently about the process of turning that desire into reality; I look at each possibility and simulate the whole process in my mind. Just as chess players run tens of thousands of possible moves through their heads, I repeatedly think through the entire process of working toward my goal, eliminating any ineffective strategies my mind devises and revising and reworking my plan each time. If I stick tenaciously to this process, I begin to see the path toward success as if it were a road I have taken before. What was at first just a dream comes closer and closer to reality until there is no longer any distinction between the two and I can paint the successful realization of the idea in minute detail in my mind. I see it taking place before my eyes not in monochrome but in vivid color. This process is similar to image training in sports: The thought becomes so concentrated that the athlete can see it as a crystallization of reality.

On the other hand, if we don't desire a certain outcome strongly enough, if we don't think about it deeply enough, and if we don't tackle it squarely until we can visualize precisely what it will look like when it is achieved, we will have little hope of finding success in creative work or in life. When one is developing a new product, for example, it is not enough to create a device that fulfills certain preexisting specifications or features certain functions that other devices already provide. If the product developer fails to establish ideal criteria for the new product that have been forged through this process of deep thought, the end product will always be of inferior quality, even if it fulfills the clients' specifications. Because it has been developed according to "sensible" standards, the end product will fail to appeal to a broader market.

I am reminded of one of our researchers, a graduate of an elite university in Japan. He spent months developing a new product, but when he showed it to me, I took one look and said, "It's not good enough."

"What do you mean?" he demanded. "It's exactly what the customers want."

"I was expecting something better," I told him. "And it's such a boring color."

"How can you be so irrational?" he protested. "You're an engineer. This is an industrial product. Color isn't important. Your criteria are unscientific."

"You can call me irrational if you like, but this is not what I envisioned." I insisted that he try again, fully aware of how angry he would be at me for rejecting his work after all that effort. I rejected his product, however, because I could see that it did not match the image I had forged for it in my mind. As a result of repeated attempts, he and his project team then succeeded in producing the ideal product.

My parents frequently used the expression "so sharp it cuts the hand" to describe something so exquisite that one can't find fault with it. When a product reaches that level of perfection, awe and admiration make us almost afraid to touch it. If we want to reach the pinnacle of the creative process, we must spare no effort in the quest for this kind of perfection.

Dreams Come True When You Can Visualize Every Detail

When we want to achieve a goal, regardless of whether it is work related or applies to any other aspect of our lives, we always should strive to realize it in its ideal form, maintaining a strong focus on thinking the goal through until we can visualize it. This process is essential if we are to realize our dreams. If we set our sights high and strive until reality converges with our ideal, we will get the results we want. Goals that are clearly visualized right from the start produce results so sharp that they cut the hand. Conversely, if we do not clearly visualize our goals, we may attain them, but the end results will not be sharp. I have experienced this time and again in my life.

When DDI (now KDDI) entered the cell phone business, for example, I declared to the other executives that we were entering the age of the cell phone. In the near future, I announced, communication will take place anywhere, anytime, with anyone. Moreover, I insisted, all people, from children to the elderly, will have their own phone numbers. Although the other executives shook their heads and laughed in disbelief, I could see already how the cell phone, a product with limitless possibilities, would spread—and I even could see how quickly this transition would happen. I had a clear picture, right down to pricing, product size, marketing strategy, and distribution.

As a result of my work in the semiconductor business and with other Kyocera ventures, I had witnessed the speed of technical innovations and the limitless extent of developments in product size and cost. My work background gave me enough experiential knowledge to predict with considerable accuracy the expansion of the cell phone market. In fact, I concretely anticipated not only the breadth of market expansion but also future fee rates. The general manager in charge of DDI at that time took notes during the meeting at which I forecast these market events. Later, when the cell phone business was launched, he looked back over those notes and found that amazingly, the fee rates were almost exactly what I had predicted.

The price of any product is determined only after making complex and detailed calculations that take into consideration factors such as the balance of demand and supply and investment recovery, yet I was able to visualize even the service charge before any calculations had been made. The general manager was stunned by my accuracy, but this is a prime example of the power of visualization. You will always be able to realize whatever you visualize clearly. What you can see in your mind, you can do; what you can't see, you can't do. If you desire a specific outcome, you must concentrate on its realization with a fierce tenacity until it becomes a passionate desire, at which point you will be able to see what success looks like in minute detail.

The fact that we can desire to be a certain way or achieve a certain outcome is in itself proof that we have the inherent capacity to make our wishes into reality. People usually can't imagine what they aren't capable of doing. If you can visualize yourself attaining a particular goal—if, when you close your eyes and imagine success, you can see the image clearly—you probably are capable of achieving it.

Success Requires Scrupulous Effort and Preparation

When you attempt something new, something that never has been done before, you are bound to meet with opposition. If, however, you attempt a new venture while maintaining an inner conviction that it can be done and can visualize its successful realization clearly, you should be able to move ahead boldly and develop your idea. Ideas should be based on an audacious optimism that spreads the wings of inspiration. To do this, it is helpful to surround yourself with optimists who will encourage leaps of the imagination.

During DDI's infancy, whenever I had an inspiration, I would call the executives together to get their opinions. I found that the more elite the university a person had graduated from was, the cooler his or her reaction was and the more likely he or she was to lecture me on how rash my proposal was. Of course, there was truth in what they were saying and their analysis was astute, but if every new idea is greeted with a cold barrage of logical reasons for why it can't succeed, in the end, even a good idea will wither, and even the possible will become impossible.

After several experiences like this, I decided to bounce my ideas off of a different group of people. Instead of smart, analytical people who approach new and difficult work cautiously and pessimistically, I chose those who greeted my suggestions with innocent enthusiasm and approval, even if my proposals were slightly scatterbrained. This may sound reckless, but when you are developing an idea, surrounding yourself with this degree of optimism is just right.

Such bold optimism, however, is effective only when one first is developing an idea or concept. When you enter the planning stage, you must base the concrete content of your idea on pessimism, assess the risk factors, and develop it carefully and cautiously. Then, once you are ready to begin actual implementation, you should switch back to optimism and set to work with confidence. To transform our thoughts into reality we need to conceive optimistically, plan pessimistically, and execute optimistically.

Along these same lines, Mitsuro Oba, the first person to trek solo across both the north and south poles, once told me something very helpful about how he readies himself for his journeys. Kyocera had provided various products for Oba's treks, and he came to my office to thank us. I immediately praised him for his courage in undertaking such dangerous adventures, but he looked uncomfortable. "Actually, I'm not courageous at all," he told me. "In fact, I'm a complete coward. But because I'm afraid, I prepare really carefully for these journeys. That's probably why I succeeded again this time, too. If an adventurer is just bold and not cautious, it will be the death of him."

When I heard this, I realized that regardless of their field, people who succeed have a firm grasp on the truths of life. Courage that is not backed by fear, caution, and meticulousness is merely reckless valor.

Learning from Illness

Up to this point I have shared with you a fundamental principle of life: The way we think can change our lives. I myself, however, learned this only through repeated mistakes, setbacks, and difficulties. When I was young, it seemed that everything that could go wrong for me would go wrong. I could not understand why nothing ever seemed to go the way I hoped, and I felt abandoned by God or fortune—an unlucky man. Unhappy with everything, I frequently became cynical and resentful of the world. But as I struggled my way through repeated setbacks, it gradually dawned on me that my own mind was the cause of all my hardships.

The first setback I confronted was my failure to pass the entrance exams for junior high school. To make matters worse, I came down with tuberculosis, which at that time was considered incurable. Tuberculosis seemed to run in my family and had killed three of my grandparents. "Soon I'll vomit blood and die, too," I thought. But all I could do was lie listlessly in bed with a low-grade fever and wallow in the depths of futility and despair.

The woman living next door to my family must have felt sorry for me because she gave me a book called *The Truth of Life* by Masaharu Taniguchi, the founder of the Truth of Life Movement. Although the content of the book was a little over my head, I desperately needed something to cling to and read it eagerly. Within its pages I discovered the following concept: There is a magnet in people's minds that draws misfortune to them. When people become ill, they do so because their weak minds drew that illness to them.

I was fascinated by that idea. Taniguchi explained that everything we encounter in life is attracted by and a projection of our minds. Illness is no exception. While this concept may sound a little cruel, as I read Taniguchi's words, something clicked inside me. When my grandfather contracted tuberculosis, my family cared for him in a building attached to our home. I was so terrified of catching the disease that I would hold my nose and run whenever I had to pass that building. My father, in contrast, cared for him personally, and even my older brother seemed unconcerned for his own health, telling me that tuberculosis was not that easy to catch. I was the only one in my family who avoided my grandfather, yet in my immediate family I was the one who later contracted the disease.

Perhaps it was a punishment. My negative thinking—my aversion to the disease and desire to avoid it—actually called misfortune to me. Precisely because I feared contracting tuberculosis, I contracted it. This made me realize that a mind focused on the negative attracts a negative outcome. Taniguchi's words made me acutely aware that the image in my mind indeed became my reality. Reflecting on my actions, I promptly vowed to think only positive thoughts from then on. It's not easy, however, to change your way of thinking, and I frequently strayed from the path of positivity.

Your Destiny Depends on Your State of Mind

Fortunately, I was cured of tuberculosis and returned to school, but I continued to be plagued by setbacks. I failed to gain entrance into my university of choice. Although I entered a local university and did well in my studies, the country suddenly plunged into a recession after a decline in the Korean War procurement boom. I had no connections, and my job applications were repeatedly turned down. Few companies were willing to let a graduate from a new rural university even apply for a job, and I cursed my bad luck and the unfairness of the world.

Why, I wondered, am I so unlucky? If I buy a lottery ticket, the persons in front of and behind me may win, but I never will. If I'm just going to fail anyway, what's the point in trying? My thoughts grew increasingly pessimistic. I had done some karate and was moderately good at it, and I began toying with the idea of joining the yakuza. I even hung around for a time in front of a gang office in a busy shopping district.

Through the efforts of one of my professors, I eventually managed to get a job with a ceramics company in Kyoto, but the firm was on the verge of bankruptcy. Our wages frequently were paid late, and to make matters worse, the company managers were squabbling among themselves. Although I finally had landed a job, I found my situation discouraging. Understandably, whenever we newly hired employees happened upon one another, we immediately started complaining and talking about quitting. First one of my coworkers quit and then another, until finally I was the only one left.

Once my situation reached this stage, I had no choice but to put my negative thoughts about my job behind me. There was no point complaining any further about my circumstances, so I decided to change my approach to my job completely. I threw myself into my research, working as hard as I could. I even moved my cooking pots to the lab so that I didn't have to go home to eat and could instead concentrate solely on conducting experiments.

My work began to reflect my change in attitude, and I produced results that earned the praise of my superiors. Their recognition made me want to work even harder, which consequently produced even better results, creating a positive cycle. In the end, I succeeded in developing Japan's first synthetic fine ceramic material for television picture tubes, using my own original scientific methodology. My accomplishment brought me even greater recognition from my superiors. I now found my work so interesting and meaningful that I no longer cared whether my salary was paid on time. Moreover, the skills I acquired and the results I obtained at a job I initially detested became the foundation for the subsequent success of Kyocera.

From the moment I changed my attitude, my life changed, and I was able to break a vicious circle and replace it with a constructive cycle. This experience convinced me that a person's destiny is not predetermined. Rather, we have the power in the form of our own volition to achieve positive or negative outcomes in our lives. The many difficulties I experienced in my youth helped me realize a basic principle: Our minds generate everything that happens in our lives, and the hardships of my younger years made me see that this truth penetrates all aspects of our lives. The events in our lives all sprout from seeds we sow. Even those who believe they have carved their own destiny through their actions alone actually have generated all the ups and downs in their lives by what they visualized in their minds.

Although destiny does exist, it is not a predetermined fate that is fixed in stone. Rather, our attitude can change the course of our lives. In fact, the human mind is the only thing that can change destiny—we make our own lives. In Japanese thought, this is called *ritsumei*: aligning one's course of life with the ultimate reality. On the canvas of life, each person paints his or her own picture, using the pigments of his or her thoughts. The color of your life is determined by the image in your mind.

13

If You Never Give Up, Success Is Guaranteed

People who meet with success in their lives when they attempt new ventures are people who sincerely believe in their potential. *Potential* means "future ability." If we judge our inherent ability by what we can do in the present, we will never be able to achieve anything new or rise above a new challenge. When we believe in our potential and set a goal that exceeds the current level of our ability, we must keep our desire to achieve it constantly burning, focusing all our energy on attaining that goal in the future. This leads to success and expands the realm of our capabilities.

When Kyocera received its first large parts order from IBM, the specifications of the order were incredibly strict. In an age when most specifications consisted of a single drawing, IBM's specifications were so minutely detailed and lengthy that they could fill a book. No matter how many times we tried to meet IBM's specifications, our samples were rejected. We would think, "This time we've finally done it!" only to be rejected yet again.

Not only were IBM's precision specifications a whole digit stricter than any we had encountered before, but we lacked equipment that could measure to such a degree of precision. To be honest, many times the thought passed through my mind that we didn't have the technology to do the job. However, for a small, unknown business like ours, this was a priceless opportunity to add to our proprietary technology and make our name known. I exhorted our despondent staff to devote themselves wholeheartedly to this project, to give it their best effort and use all the technology available to us, yet the results were still inadequate. After we had exhausted every possible avenue to meet the specifications of the project, I finally asked the person in charge, "Did you pray?" I wanted to be sure that all that was left was to wait for Providence to act.

Eventually, as a result of repeated superhuman effort, we succeeded in developing a "sharp" product that met IBM's specifications and then kept our plant running at full capacity for two years to deliver an enormous volume of products to IBM on time. As I watched as the last truckload of goods from the project was driven away, I was struck by the thought that human ability is limitless. If we direct all our passion toward accomplishing what looks like an impossible goal and strive single-mindedly to achieve it, our capacity will expand phenomenally. The effort will awaken our latent abilities and cause them to flower. It is therefore essential to think in the future tense: The person I am right now may not be able to do this, but my future self can do it. We must believe that untapped powers lie dormant within us.

When I accepted the IBM job on behalf of Kyocera, I knew that its skill requirements far surpassed the technical level of our company. In that sense, it was a reckless promise. That, however, was my normal approach. From the early days of our company, I frequently accepted jobs that major manufacturers had turned down because they thought the projects were too difficult. For a new and minor company with no track record, accepting these jobs was often the only way to get work. Of course, there was no guarantee that we could succeed at a job considered too difficult by major companies with more advanced technology, but I never used the word *can't*. I didn't even say we might be able to do it. I always stated emphatically that we could.

Whenever I announced a new project to my staff, they invariably responded with dismay, but I was always convinced that we would be able to see it through to completion. I made sure to suggest ways in which it could be done and passionately communicated what a positive impact it would have on our company in the hopes that everyone involved in the project would rise enthusiastically to the challenge. Whenever they confronted difficulties, I would tell them, "Impossible is just one stop on the road to success. I know we can do this if we give it everything we've got and stick with it to the end."

Perhaps it was dishonest to tell our clients that I could do something that seemed impossible. But when we start from a place of seeming impossibility and strive diligently and passionately until there is nothing left to do but wait for Providence to extend a helping hand, success transforms that rash promise into the truth. By thinking of my ability in the future tense, I have succeeded repeatedly in realizing the impossible.

15

Repeated Effort Makes the Ordinary Extraordinary

Kazuo Murakami, professor emeritus at the University of Tsukuba and a recognized authority on genetics, gives a very simple explanation for the "inhuman" strength some people are able to muster in emergency situations. An extraordinary potential for strength exists within human beings, but because the gene that governs that strength is switched off, it is usually dormant. When it is switched on, however, we can access extraordinary strength even at ordinary times. Moreover, he claims that positive thinking and a constructive mental attitude greatly increase our ability to activate the switch that governs our innate yet dormant abilities. Genetic research thus validates the concept that one's attitude has the power to expand one's potential greatly.

But what is our potential? From the perspective of genetics, anything we can imagine, anything we think we want, is within the realm of possibility. In other words, we possess an innate ability to realize our aspirations. It is essential, however, not only to set our aims high but also to strive to reach the goals we set through consistent, steady effort.

When Kyocera was just a small factory with less than a hundred employees, I boldly declared that our company would become the best in the world. I did not think of this aspiration as a distant dream but rather as a passionate desire that I was determined to achieve. However, no matter how high we set our sights, we also need to keep our feet firmly on the ground. Although we must have high aspirations and dreams, everyday reality demands that we exert our utmost effort in simple, steady work, overcoming the problems that confront us one by one so that we can move one step farther ahead than we were yesterday.

Many times I wondered if Kyocera would ever reach the top and felt overwhelmed by the gap between my dream for the company and reality. But life is, after all, the sum of all our todays, the continuation of now. The accumulation of each second becomes a day; the accumulation of each day becomes a week, a month, a year; and before we realize it, we are standing on a pinnacle that once seemed unreachable. That is life.

Even if we are in a hurry to greet what the future brings, tomorrow will not come until we have lived this day. There is no shortcut to the destination we have painted in our minds. A great distance can be traveled only one step at a time, and a great dream is reached little by little, day by day. If we live each day fully and earnestly rather than wasting it, tomorrow will come into view. If we put our full effort into the next day that comes, a week will come into view. And if we live that week fully, we will begin to catch sight of a month. . . . In other words, if we concentrate all our energy on living each moment instead of constantly trying to rush ahead, the future will become visible without our straining to see it.

That is the pace at which I have lived my life: slow and steady, like the tortoise that beat the hare. It was through steady, accumulated effort that Kyocera grew into what it is today and I went from an unknown engineer to a respected businessman. It is far better to devote your efforts to living fully every second of every day than to waste time worrying about tomorrow or focusing your thoughts on trying to read the future. In the end, this is the best way to realize your dreams.

Daily Innovations Lead to Dramatic Progress

I don't have a very high opinion of clever men because they tend to neglect today. Their intelligence allows them to foresee the future, but just like the hare, they seek the quickest route to their destination, when instead they should be living each day slowly but surely like the tortoise. In their impatience to achieve success, they often trip and fall. Many brilliant people have begun working at Kyocera only to quit because they believed our company had no future. Those who remained at the company were ordinary people, not particularly smart or astute and not sharp enough to change jobs. Yet many times I have witnessed these slow thinkers rise to managerial positions and become company leaders after 10 or 20 years.

It is the ability to plod away without complaint, to never give up, to continuously do one's best each day, that transforms ordinary people into extraordinary people. It is such extraordinarily ordinary people who make their dreams reality and achieve their goals by working step by step, day by day, earnestly and steadily, without seeking an easy way out.

Continuous effort is important, but this does not mean that people should merely do the same thing over and over. Continuity and repetition are different things. Rather than mindlessly repeating what we did the day before, we should seek ways to make tomorrow better than today, always adding some improvement tomorrow to our efforts from today. This creative attitude of innovation accelerates the rate at which we can achieve success. As an engineer, I am trained to ask myself if my results are good enough or whether there is a better way. If you look at what you are doing from that perspective, there is infinite potential for innovation in even the most mundane tasks.

Take cleaning, for example. Instead of using a broom to sweep as you have always done, think about how to do it better and faster, for example, by trying a mop or requesting that money be allocated to buy a vacuum cleaner. Or you could try the various processes involved in cleaning in a different order or a different way to find the most efficient and effective way to clean. No matter how small the task, in the long run there will be a striking difference between people who approach their work with the desire to improve and people who don't. In the case of cleaning, the innovative person eventually may establish an independent company that wins contracts for large buildings whereas the person who mindlessly fills his cleaning quota without trying to improve most likely will still be cleaning.

In the end, striving daily to make little improvements makes a huge difference. The key to success is never to stick to the road you are used to traveling.

Listening for the Voice of God

God inhabits the workplace. There are times in our work when despite many attempts, we hit a brick wall and feel we have exhausted our every effort. When we approach these dead ends, however, we are actually arriving at the true starting point. Dead ends give us the opportunity to stop and regain our objectivity, to reassess our circumstances.

I once met Kohei Nakabo, a Japanese lawyer who argued for the plaintiff in many high-profile cases. Nakabo's cases included the suit lodged by victims of arsenic-tainted baby formula against Morinaga & Company in the 1970s and the case brought forward by investors who had been swindled out of over 200 billion yen during the Toyoda Shoji gold transaction fraud in the early 1980s. When I asked Nakabo what he thought was most essential to doing his work successfully, he responded, "All the keys to solving the case are there at the scene of the crime. God is there." Although our fields differ, the same is true for me. Nakabo's statement reaffirmed my conviction that dedicated attention to the workplace and careful observation are essential if we are to find career success.

In the manufacturing field, this means we must assess every aspect of our work, including the product, the machines, the

19

materials, the tools, and even the processes, examining them with an open and humble mind. We must do far more than physically recheck our work or return to the starting point. Rather, we must tune our whole mind and body to the product or the workplace and listen intently. If you do this, you will hear God's voice whispering hints for what to do next. I call this listening to what the product says.

Ceramic products are made by pressing powdered metal oxides into molds, which are then fired at high temperatures in kilns. This process is similar to that of making china, but the creation of ceramics requires an extremely high level of precision because the products are made for the electronics industry and therefore must be flawless. Even the slightest variation or deformity is impermissible, as it could render the electronic device unusable. When we started Kyocera, we were commissioned to develop a new ceramics product, but whenever we fired the product's molds, the material came out twisted and warped. After much trial and error, we realized that our approach to pressing the material into the molds had resulted in different densities in the top and bottom of the material, causing it to warp.

Although we had identified the cause of the warping, it was very difficult to find a way to achieve uniform density in the product. We tried a variety of methods without success. Wanting to see just what was happening inside the kiln when we fired the material, I opened a peephole and settled down to watch. As the temperature rose, the material began to twist and turn, as if it were alive. Every time we tried to fire the material, the same thing happened. I could hardly bear to watch. I wanted to shout, "Stop twisting!" and was overcome by an urge to thrust my hand in and hold the material down, even though I knew that the temperature in the kiln exceeded 1,000 degrees Centigrade. That was how much this product meant to me, a feeling sparked not only by my passionate involvement in the product as an engineer but also by my knowledge that our company could not afford any losses. As it turned out, however, my urge to press down on the material led to a solution, and I realized that it was the product's response to my urgent need. When we tried firing the product with a heat-resistant weight on top, it emerged from the kiln completely flat.

Through such experiences, I have come to believe that the answers we seek already exist in the workplace. To obtain them, we must have passion and intensity for our work that are stronger than anyone else's. We also must observe with clarity and patience. Only when we incline our ears and hearts to the product and keep our gaze fixed on it will we hear what the product has to say and find the right solution.

I know it sounds very unscientific, but in my experience, what we think of as inorganic matter, such as a product or the workplace, responds to the depth of our feeling and the keenness of our observations by coming alive and speaking in a wordless voice. When matter responds to the heart, we can accomplish our aim, which in the field of manufacturing is the development of sharp products.

Always Pay Voluntary Attention

The Kyocera Group makes printers and copy machines that use light-sensitive amorphous silicon drums. These drums are far harder and, consequently, have an exceptionally longer life span than conventional products. They can be used continuously without needing to be replaced for the life of the machine (10 times longer than conventional drums), which makes them much better for the environment.

Kyocera was the first company to mass-produce these drums. They are made by applying a silicon film to the surface of a polished aluminum tube. The film must be applied evenly to achieve the necessary sensitivity, but doing so is extremely difficult. Any unevenness, even a discrepancy of 0.001 millimeter, is unacceptable. Three years after we began research and development of the drums, we succeeded in evenly applying the film just once but were unable to repeat the process. This meant that the technology was not suited to mass production.

At the time, many other companies around the world were involved in the same research, but no one else had succeeded in mass-producing the drums either. I was close to giving up but decided to try one last time, going back to the starting line and taking a close look at the production site. I was sure that if we watched every event or change that occurred during the process of making the film, we could catch something and hear what the product had to say. I ordered the researchers in charge to pay close attention to every little detail and everything that happened during the production process, no matter how insignificant.

One night when I dropped in on a researcher who should have been carefully observing the manufacturing process, I found him nodding off in his chair. Instead of hearing what the product had to say, all I could hear was snoring. I replaced him with someone who I knew was a keen observer. I also moved Kyocera's laboratory from Kagoshima to Shiga and made significant staff changes, appointing a new leader of the group and promoting many newcomers. Overhauling the entire research team, which had been a fixed group for several years, was a big risk, but it turned out to be a highly successful move, and within one year we had achieved mass production of the drum. The new team had what the original team lacked: a deep attachment to its work and the product and the passion to conduct thorough on-site observations. It takes this kind of rigorous dedication to create new and superior products.

There is a Japanese expression, "voluntary attention." It means to consciously pay attention, to have a goal and focus your whole consciousness, every nerve in your body, on that goal. When we hear a noise and look toward it, that is a reflexive biological response; in other words, it is involuntary attention. In contrast, voluntary attention entails focusing our awareness intentionally on everything around us, no matter how insignificant the detail. The type of observation my team at Kyocera employed in refining the mass production process of the drum requires this kind of continuous voluntary attention. It is not enough merely to gaze absently at the object or to drift off.

The philosopher Tempu Nakamura, whom I mentioned in the prologue, once said that "life is meaningless unless it is lived with voluntary attention." Our concentration span is limited, making it difficult to focus our attention on one thing. If we keep striving to maintain our focus, however, we gradually will develop the habit of voluntary attention and the ability to grasp the essence of things, and we will be able to make accurate judgments.

23

In the past, when I was busy, I used to stop my employees in the hall to catch up on their progress or pass on instructions, but that practice caused problems later. Employees would claim that they had told me something even though I was sure they hadn't. After a few such experiences, I decided to make time to listen to my employees in a room or a corner of the office where I could concentrate on what they said.

Voluntary attention is like a drill. A drill is most effective when all its force is concentrated on one point. If we concentrate all our attention on our goal, which is equivalent to the point of a drill, we will achieve it. Concentration is generated by the strength, depth, and size of our thoughts. Everything that has ever been accomplished began with the desire to make it happen. Our success or failure depends on how passionately and constantly we can maintain that desire and how earnestly we can work toward realizing our goal.

Dream Ambitiously and Succeed in Life

So far we have looked at understanding the power of desire and consciously utilizing it. The foundation for exploiting this power and making great achievements in work and life is to dream big dreams. Dream. Be ambitious. Yearn passionately.

Some people will counter that it is hard enough just to get through every day, that they don't have time to dream or hope. But the dreams of people who have the strength to make their lives their own are extremely ambitious; they invariably desire things that are beyond their reach. The same is true for me. The driving force that brought me as far as I have come was the greatness of my dreams and goals.

As I mentioned earlier, when I established Kyocera, I aimed to make it the leading manufacturer of ceramics in the world and repeatedly shared that dream with my employees. I had no concrete strategy or accurate estimates for achieving that goal. At that point, it was totally unrealistic, but at every opportunity I had, I told them my dream. Through this process, my dream became the aspiration of our entire staff, and that led to its realization.

No dream can be achieved if we never dream it, and only the dreams that we long to attain are attainable. Kyocera eventually became the top company in our field because our desire was so intense that it penetrated our subconscious minds, because we voiced our dream and united our actions toward realizing it. The greater the dream, the longer it may take to realize. However, if we repeatedly visualize what our dream will look like when it is achieved, if we repeatedly simulate in vivid color the process of reaching it, we will begin to see how to get there and will discover many ideas for attaining it even within the routine of daily life.

There are times when the inspiration for realizing a dream comes unexpectedly from a seemingly insignificant event in our lives, such as walking down the street, relaxing over a cup of tea, or talking with a friend. Different people can experience or see the same thing, but many will miss the inspirational hints that life offers them. The difference between those who discover important ideas and those who don't is awareness. Many people had seen an apple fall from the tree before Newton, but only he discovered within that phenomenon the law of universal gravitation. He succeeded because his passionate desire to find an answer had penetrated his subconscious.

As I mentioned earlier, if we keep the flame of longing burning, we will receive the divine inspiration that is the source of all creative achievements. Therefore, no matter how old we grow, we should always talk about our dreams and look hopefully toward the future. Without dreams, we can't create, achieve, or grow as human beings. It is through visualizing our dreams, repeatedly trying out creative innovations and exerting diligent effort, that our characters are refined. Dreams and desires are thus the springboard for life.

CHAPTER 2

THINKING IN TRUTHS AND PRINCIPLES

Simple Truths and Principles Are Best

People tend to think that things are more complex than they actually are. The essence of all things is quite simple. Even things that appear complicated are made up of simple components. Our genes, for example, consist of a whopping 3 billion chromosome sequences, but the genetic code that is used to express each sequence consists of only four chemical letters. The cloth of truth is woven with a single thread. Therefore, the more we simplify the experiences or phenomena in our lives, the closer we come to their original form—to the truth. When we confront something that appears complex, it is important to strive to break each of its parts down into as simple a form as possible. This is a law of life, and it applies to business, too.

The truths and principles of business are extremely simple. I often am asked to reveal the tricks of my trade, the secret of my success, but I can see the disappointment in the questioners' faces when I share my point of view. They are incredulous that I could manage a business with such obvious, simple, and primitive guidelines.

When I began Kyocera at the age of 27, I had some experience as an engineer but no knowledge of or background in company management. Problems arose frequently, and decisions had to be made. Because I was the president of Kyocera, it was my responsibility to make final decisions and determine the best solution to any given situation. I had to respond promptly, even when the issue pertained to a department of my company, like sales or accounting, about which I was totally ignorant. If I erred in judgment on even the smallest of Kyocera's problems, my mistake could have a direct impact on the future of the entire company. But I was an engineer, not a businessman. I had no knowledge on which to base my decisions and no experience on which to draw in determining the next step. I wondered what on earth I should do.

After much thought, I finally decided to base my decisions and actions on the simple truths and principles that generally are accepted as standards of decent human behavior. If I choose to do what is right, I thought, I should be able to continue doing the right thing to the end. All I need to do is to follow the commonsense rules for living that I learned from my parents and teachers, to tell the truth rather than lie, to be kind rather than greedy and inconsiderate, and so on.

I concluded that the moral and ethical guidelines that determine right from wrong, good deeds from bad, and permissible behavior from impermissible could be applied directly to management policy and decision-making criteria. After all, running a business involves human relationships, and therefore the same primitive ethical standards that apply to the treatment of individuals should apply to business interactions. I believed that life and business should operate according to the same truths and principles and that if I followed these guidelines, I could not go far astray—a very simple concept.

This approach gave me the confidence to play fair in all my business dealings, and I believe it is what led Kyocera to our subsequent success.

A Living Philosophy That Guides Us

The set of simple truths and principles that guide us to do what is right as human beings represents a living philosophy that is borne from experience and practice rather than from the type of convoluted reasoning that is limited to desk-bound learning. This philosophy provides the guidelines we need to find our way through uncertainty, distress, and hardship.

In life we constantly face situations in which we must make a decision. At home or at work, in the process of finding a job or getting married, we are forced to make choices. Living is the accumulation of such decisions, a continuous series of choices. The present is the result of those decisions, and the choices we make from now on will determine the rest of our lives. Having a set of truths and principles to guide us makes a huge difference in how we go about making the decisions that will set the course of our lives. Making choices without guiding principles is like navigating without a compass, and taking action without following an underlying philosophy is like walking through the dark without a light. Philosophy or, if you prefer, ethical and moral values serve as a standard for living, a place we can return to when we lose our way.

KDDI, one of the largest telecommunication carriers in Japan, was formed in late 2000 by the merger of three companies: DDI (Daini Denden), the company I originally founded; KDD (Kokusai Denshin Denwa), Japan's largest international tele-communications firm; and IDO (Nippon Idou Tsushin Corporation), a subsidiary of Toyota. Our alliance made it possible to compete with NTT (Nippon Telegraph and Telephone Corporation), a giant telecommunications company formerly owned by the Japanese government.

Prior to the merger, DDI and IDO both used the same mobile phone systems. However, because the two companies had split coverage of Japan, with each company owning only half of the country's nationwide mobile phone network, neither DDI nor IDO could ever hope to rival NTT's subsidiary, NTT DoCoMo, whose size gave NTT control in this field. That would mean that the market would never be influenced by the principle of competition, leaving NTT DoCoMo with a virtual monopoly and users without the benefits of improved services and lower costs. That is why I proposed the merger.

But what kind of merger would be appropriate? Should one of our companies absorb the others, or should each company enter the merger on equal footing? Looking at past examples of how banks and other organizations had approached equal mergers, I found when the merging parties clung to the idea of equality, they found themselves embroiled in long battles wherein each party attempted to secure its own piece of control over the new company. After much thought, I finally proposed that instead of an equal merger, DDI should lead the coalition. My suggestion did not come out of any desire for power on my part, nor did it come because I wanted to give my company an advantage. It was based on the objective assessment that of the three merging companies, DDI had the best business record and the strongest management base.

The truths and principles that guide businesses should not derive from private profit or personal fame but from contributing to people and society. Providing the public with the best products and services should be the guiding principle underpinning business management. If KDDI was to follow this principle successfully, then the merger of our three companies would not be enough. We would need to identify management responsibility clearly, ensure that the new company got on track as quickly as possible, and provide for long-term stable management. Without these essentials, we could not hope to compete and benefit the users and society.

This objective view was the basis for my conclusion that the best solution was for DDI to take the initiative and lead the merger. I frankly and sincerely shared the reasons for my proposal with the other parties involved, including my vision of what the telecommunications industry in Japan should become. I further proposed that Kyocera be given slightly more shares than Toyota even though Toyota was the largest shareholder in both IDO and KDD. Through the sincerity and passion of all involved, the merger was completed and the new company KDDI advanced rapidly. It was this principle of putting others first that led to our success.

31

Stand by Your Principles, Unmoved by Trends

Developing and adhering to a solid philosophy based on truths and principles will lead to success and a fruitful life, but this road is not fun or easy traveling. On the contrary, it is a rocky path that requires self-discipline and restraint, one that often is accompanied by suffering and sometimes by loss. When you take the rocky path and reach a crossroads, you must choose the route that leads to the right path, even if it is thorny and far removed from any personal reward, even if it means picking a clumsy and foolishly honest way of life. In the long run, however, actions based on a solid philosophy never result in loss. Despite the fact that they appear disadvantageous, in the end such genuine actions will profit you. With this approach you rarely will stray from the right path.

To illustrate this concept, consider Japan's experience during the asset price bubble, which wreaked so much havoc on the economy that its reverberations are felt to this day. During the years leading up to the bubble many companies were caught up in real estate speculation. Buying and reselling property caused land prices to skyrocket, and companies borrowed huge sums to invest in real estate in anticipation of high returns. When one logically considers the economic principles underlying the rapid inflation of Japan's asset prices, it seems very strange that the value of one's assets would increase without any effort, yet people behaved as if this phenomenon were perfectly normal. When the bubble burst, however, properties that should have been increasing in value suddenly became liabilities, and many companies found themselves heavily in debt. In retrospect, if the people in charge of the companies engaging in rampant speculation had followed a strong guiding philosophy, they would have been able to make the right decisions for their companies without being swayed by financial trends.

When land prices were still rising, many people urged Kyocera to invest the savings we had accumulated through hard work in real estate. One banker, thinking that I did not understand the advantages of real estate investing, meticulously explained how I could rake in profit. But I did not believe that huge profits could be obtained by merely moving land from one hand to another. Even if it was true that profit could be gained so easily, I had not earned that profit. I rejected those offers because I believed money that comes easily also vanishes easily. True profit, I was convinced, is made through honest hard work.

It was a simple tenet, but it was based on the guiding principles that determine right behavior. Although I needed to exercise self-discipline to resist greed, I was able to keep my heart from getting wrapped up in tales of huge investment profits. Thus, the attainment of true success, which is gained only through rightful living, depends on whether you have a philosophy worth upholding regardless of loss and whether you have the commitment to accept the suffering that choice entails.

To Know Is Not Enough: Live Your Philosophy

Living according to a guiding philosophy is easier said than done. As human beings, we easily succumb to temptation and selfish desires unless we are very strong and disciplined.

Many years ago, after Kyocera had given executives the use of a company car and driver, one executive found that the car was unavailable when he wanted to go home. Assuming that the executive would be working late, the person in charge of general affairs had let a very busy sales manager take the company car to his appointments that day. Furious, the executive demanded to know why a lowly sales manager should be allowed to use the company car.

When the incident came to my attention, I called the executive to my office. "You weren't given the use of a car because of your rank," I told him. "We decided to provide this service to allow people who perform particularly important work for the company to concentrate on their jobs without being burdened by routine tasks. Think about it. You wanted to use the car to go home at the end of regular working hours. As an executive, do you really have the right to criticize the sales manager for using the car to get to all his business appointments on time?"

Although an executive may have first priority for its use, the car still belongs to the company, not to the individual. It is difficult, however, for people in high positions to see the situation through this lens. I know because I've done the same thing myself. At the time of Kyocera's establishment, the company vehicle was a scooter, which I naturally drove myself. Later I upgraded to a tiny Subaru 360, which in the beginning I also drove myself. But I realized that as I was driving, I was thinking of work the whole time, and after grasping how dangerous this was, I hired a chauffeur. Eventually, Kyocera could afford to buy a bigger car, and I was driven to work every day. One morning my wife was leaving on an errand just as the car pulled up, and I offered her a lift. She refused: "If it were your car, I'd say yes, but that's the company car. It was you who told me that people shouldn't use the company car for personal errands and insisted that we clearly separate personal and business matters." She was right, of course, and what she said helped me reflect on my actions.

Although these are trivial examples, they illustrate the fact that many things are easier said than done. This is why truths and principles are meaningless if we do not pursue them with a strong will. Although they are the wellspring of right behavior and strength, they are easily forgotten if we lack discipline. We should always remember to reflect on our actions and exercise self-control. It is important to incorporate these habits within our guidelines for living.

The Vector of Attitude Determines the Direction of Your Life

The lessons I have learned through my work and my management experience, the simple principles for living, all seem very ordinary. However, I believe that simplicity is closely related to universality. In this chapter, I share a few of these basic principles.

The first principle I want to discuss is my formula for living, which I introduced in the Prologue: The results we achieve from work and life = attitude × effort × ability. The most important factor in this equation is attitude. I developed this formula when I was trying to discover how someone like me with only mediocre talent could achieve the extraordinary and thereby help others and society. Ever since I created it, this formula has been the basis for my way of life.

The key to this equation is that its results are obtained through multiplication. For example, if someone scores 90 out of 100 for her ability to think clearly but then becomes proud of that ability, fails to work hard, and scores only 30 out of a 100 for her effort, the end product of her work will be only 2,700. In contrast, what happens when a person with an average thinking ability of only 60 works extra hard to compensate for what he lacks and devotes more than 90 percent of his effort to his work? The end result is 5,400 points. The person who makes the greater effort, therefore, can do twice as much with his work as can the person who does not try with hers.

A person's score is also multiplied by attitude. Attitude is of the utmost importance, because it determines the orientation of our lives. There are people who focus their efforts and ability in a positive direction and people who focus them in a negative direction. Attitude is therefore the only factor in the equation that has both plus and minus values. If your way of thinking is negative, regardless of how high you score on effort and ability, the end result of this equation (i.e., the result of your life or your work) will be a negative value. Very talented people who direct their efforts toward fraud or theft may work very hard at their "occupation," but because their attitude toward life is negative, they will never obtain good results.

Because the factors in this formula are multiplied and therefore have a direct bearing on one another, we must strive to turn our thoughts in the right direction. Otherwise, our ability and effort, no matter how great, will go to waste and may even harm society. In a lecture he gave late in life, Yukichi Fukuzawa (1835–1901), a scholar and educator, described what makes a truly great person. According to Fukuzawa, we can reach maturity and contribute to society only when we have acquired the deep thinking of a philosopher, the pure heart of a warrior, the keen intelligence of a minor official, and the hardy physique of a farmer. When I read Fukuzawa's words, it strikes me that what he refers to as deep thinking and a pure heart correspond to attitude in my formula for living, cleverness corresponds to ability, and a strong, hardy physique corresponds to effort. Thus, his words confirm the importance of attitude, ability, and effort in our lives.

Producing the Drama Called Life

Live each day earnestly. This is another simple guideline, but it too provides a vital foundation for living. The Japanese word for earnest living is *shinken*, and in the practice of kendo (Japanese swordsmanship), *shinken* means practicing with a real blade instead of a bamboo sword. In archery, *shinken* means drawing the bow so taut that there is no slack and then, in that intense moment of concentration, releasing the arrow. Living earnestly means maintaining intensity and dedication every day in one's work and life. When we do this, we can achieve the life we envision.

Life is a drama in which each of us plays a starring role. We also serve as our own directors and scriptwriters. In fact, we have no choice but to write and play our own parts. Therefore, the most important question of existence is how to produce this drama called life. We must think about what story we want to spend our lives writing and how we wish to perform (live) our part. There is nothing more wasteful than failing to make an effort and instead spending our lives being aimless and idle. To create a satisfying drama that is rich in content, we need to approach every second of every day with complete earnestness.

When we approach all aspects of our lives with burning passion and enthusiasm, when we live with complete earnestness, the sum of our efforts becomes our worth and our lives bear fruit and reach fulfillment.

Conversely, no matter how talented we are or how good our attitude is, if we lack earnest effort, our lives will be barren. No matter how elaborate our life's script, it takes passionate dedication to make the story of our life into reality. We have the choice to confront problems that require a solution or to avoid them, and what we choose will determine our success or failure. An attitude of earnestness will keep us from avoiding the challenges that confront us.

If you maintain an urgent desire to succeed and remain humble and open-minded in your approach to life's problems, you will begin to see hints for solutions that you ordinarily would overlook. I call these hints the whisperings of revelation; it's as if God, seeing us desperately striving toward a goal, takes pity on us and gives us the answer we need. I often appeal to my employees to work so hard that God will want to help them. The spirit of squarely confronting difficulties and stretching ourselves to the limit helps us break through seemingly impossible situations and generate creative results. The accumulation of these efforts makes the ideal image we have envisioned for our lives into reality.

Nothing Is Gained without Hard Work

Another important principle of life is to value experience over knowledge. What you know is not necessarily equivalent to what you can do. This is a warning: Do not think you are capable just because you know something.

From books, we can learn that to make ceramics we need to combine certain materials and fire them at a certain temperature.

But even if we follow the instructions to the letter, the process will not turn out the way that we expect it to. It is only after gaining experience on the shop floor that we begin to grasp the essence of ceramic production. Only when experience is added to knowledge can we really "do" anything. Until that point we only "know."

With the advent of the information age, society has placed an increasing amount of emphasis on knowledge, and a broadening number of people believe that if they know, they can do. This is a major misunderstanding. There is in fact a huge difference between knowing how to do something and actually being able to do it. Only experience in the workplace can fill the gap between the two.

Just after I had established Kyocera I heard about a management seminar. It was a three-day event at a hot springs resort and the price was very high, but one of the instructors was Soichiro Honda, the founder of Honda Motor Co. Desperately wanting to hear what he had to say, I signed up against the advice of my colleagues.

On the day of his talk, the participants relaxed in the hot springs, changed into house robes provided by the hotel, and gathered in a large hall to wait for Honda. He appeared soon afterward. Having come straight from the factory, he was dressed in oil-stained coveralls. The first thing he said in his crisp, articulate voice was, "What are you doing here? They told me you want to learn about management, but if you have time to do that, the first thing you should do is get back to work right now. You can't learn about management by having a bath and lounging around eating and drinking. I'm living proof. I never learned management from anyone ever. If even I can run a company, then there is only one thing for you to do. Go back and get to work."

After rebuking us roundly, he clinched his remarks by saying, "How could you be so stupid as to pay for something like this?"

We were speechless. He was absolutely right. Captivated by his character, I resolved to go back early and start working.

Honda was trying to make us see that learning without doing is like learning to swim on dry land. It can't be done. The only way to learn is to leap into the water and start paddling. In the same way, we can't hope to manage a business without working on the shop floor. The wisdom to achieve great things can be gained only through cumulative experience, and the experience we acquire through personal involvement is the most precious asset we have.

Live Earnestly in the Moment

The best way to forge a path to the future is to live with overflowing passion and strive earnestly in the here and now, to immerse ourselves in the task before us and devote ourselves to fully utilizing each second we spend on this planet.

It may come as a surprise to many people to hear that I have never made a long-term management plan. Although I understand the importance of long-term management strategies that are based on management theory, I believe that we must live this day before tomorrow can come. If we don't know what tomorrow will bring, how can we predict what will happen in 5 or 10 years? I believe it is more important to live this day, today, as earnestly as possible. No matter how grand our goals may be, we cannot achieve them without striving daily and gradually building on our achievements. Great results are obtained only through steady effort. Future success comes about naturally when we do our best to live each day sincerely. It is this principle that I have followed as my management strategy, and experience has taught me the fundamental importance of this truth. If we live today completely, tomorrow will come into sight.

Our lives are precious. To spend our days idly doing nothing not only is a shameful waste but also flouts the will of the universe. Nature brought us into existence because we have a role to play. No one was created by accident, and therefore nothing that exists is worthless. Compared with the scale of the universe, our existence as individuals may seem insignificant, but we are here because we are needed. Every individual life, no matter how small it may be, along with every inanimate object, exists because the universe recognized its value.

All the workings of nature silently reflect the importance of living earnestly in the moment. Look at the tundra in the far north. In summer it is covered with tiny flowers. Despite the shortness of the season, those plants spend their brief lives flowering and bearing as many seeds as they can in order to pass life on to the generation that will bloom after the long winter. They waste no time on idle thoughts but simply live earnestly in the moment.

In the deserts of Africa, it rains only once or twice a year, but when it does, plants immediately sprout buds and blossoms. Within a week or two they bear seeds that fall and lie patiently in the hot sand. When the rains come again, the seeds spring to life, a new generation. Clearly, in the world of nature, all living things live each day and each precious second fully, and as a result, their small lives are connected to tomorrow. If even plants and flowers seize each moment they're given, we too should strive to fully utilize our time and not waste a single moment. This is our contract with the universe that brought us into being and continually gives our lives meaning. It is a prerequisite to living the drama of our lives the way we want.

Fire Yourself Up by Loving What You Do

There are three basic types of matter: combustible, noncombustible, and spontaneously combustible. Combustible material burns when exposed to flame, whereas noncombustible material does not. Spontaneously combustible material has the ability to burn on its own.

People can be classified in the same way that matter is. Some people get fired up with enthusiasm without any input from the people around them, whereas others remain nihilistic and impassive no matter how much energy they are exposed to. Lacking passion and enthusiasm, noncombustible people usually fail to make good use of their abilities. There is no need for noncombustible people in an organization. Not only are they personally as cold as ice, their coldness can rob others of their heat.

This is why I often tell my employees, "We don't need non-combustible people in this company. Strive to become the type of person who gets fired up on your own or at least the type of person that is capable of catching the flame when exposed to someone else's enthusiasm."

People who are achievers are those who get fired up on their own and share their energy with the people around them. They are not the type to do only what they are told, nor do they wait for instructions before they take action. They take the initiative and set out to accomplish great deeds before they are asked, and in this way they serve as a model to others. They are very proactive and constructive in their approach to their lives and their work.

But how can we become spontaneously combustible people? How can we acquire an enthusiastic nature? The best way is to fall in love with one's work. This is how I explain it to our employees: Working requires tremendous energy, an energy that arises from getting fired up. The best way to get fired up is to love your work. No matter what your job is, if you put your heart and soul into it, you will gain satisfaction and self-confidence and want to set out to achieve the next goal. As you repeat this process, achieving goal after goal, you will come to love your work even more, and eventually, no effort will seem painful and you will be able to achieve wonderful results.

Love is the greatest motivator, the mother of enthusiasm, and effort is the road to success. This concept is expressed best by the Japanese proverbs "A thousand miles seem like one when traveling for love" and "Love leads to mastery." When we love what we do, we naturally feel enthusiastic about it and want to give it our best effort, which consequently helps us improve very quickly. We even begin to look forward to doing things that others see as the most tedious chores.

I was always so busy with work that I rarely went home. It got to the point where my neighbors asked my wife when on earth I came home and her parents wrote a letter warning me that I would ruin my health through overworking myself. But they had no reason to worry because I was doing what I liked. I did not find my work difficult, and it did not tire me out either. If I had not loved my work to that extent, it would have been impossible for me to achieve excellence in it. Regardless of their field of work, successful people are those who love what they do. Falling in love with your work is a great way to enrich your life.

Overcome Yourself and Transform Your Life

What about people who just can't seem to fall in love with their work? They should begin by dedicating themselves to their work, which will incite joy to shine through the hardships they experience. To love and to devote oneself to something are like opposite sides of the same coin: There is a causal relationship between the two. You devote yourself to your work because you love it, and conversely, you come to love your work by devoting yourself to it. Even if it seems difficult to do so at first, I suggest that you keep telling yourself what a wonderful job you have and how lucky you are to be in this line of work. If you do this, the way you see your work will change naturally.

No matter what kind of work you do, if you put your heart and soul into it, you will get results and gradually will begin to enjoy it and find it interesting. This consequently will increase your enthusiasm for your work and eventually lead to good results. Within this positive cycle, you soon will notice that you have come to like your work.

As I mentioned earlier, the company I worked for after graduating from university was in such bad shape that it was in danger of folding. My coworkers quit one after the other until I was the only employee remaining in my department. When the situation got to that point, I decided there was nothing left for me to do but devote myself to completing the tasks before me. To my surprise, as soon as I began to devote myself to my work, my research results began to improve markedly. Naturally, when this occurred my work became more interesting, and that further fanned the flame of my enthusiasm, creating a positive spiral.

When you think you can't stand your work anymore, it's worth trying a little harder. Accepting your situation and adopting a positive attitude as you grapple with a problem can transform your life. Overcoming yourself is the key to accomplishing this. You must suppress your selfish desires and deal sternly with any thoughts of self-indulgence. If you can't overcome yourself, you will never succeed at anything and will never tap into your maximum potential.

Take, for example, a person with average ability who studies very hard and receives high marks and another person who is very bright and gets average marks without studying at all. The naturally brighter person may think, "That other person gets good marks because she's always studying. But if I put my mind to it, I'd do even better." After graduation, if the naturally brighter person runs into a successful businesswoman who excels through hard work, he will tell himself, "She was just an average student. I did far better than she ever did," implying that his ability is superior to hers. He may be right if we look only at innate ability, but there is a world of difference between the two people's attitudes and enthusiasm for their work. According to my formula for living, this difference reverses the results of their lives.

Someone who studies hard must sacrifice the time she otherwise would spend watching movies or television; she must struggle against the urge to take an easier path. Similarly, success in business results from a person's ability to work diligently and control his desire to take the easiest course. People who view hard workers with contempt are hiding behind their own laziness and procrastination. Their perspective on earnest endeavor is warped.

A person with true ability has the self-control to approach his work with simple honesty. Someone who succumbs to herself and avoids hard work, regardless of how much talent she was born with, lacks the ability to develop and utilize her innate capacity for greatness. A person needs more than the sum of his brain cells to be able to perform at his best and produce great results on the vast stage of life. He will succeed only when he throws himself into his work and confronts difficulties head-on. We should keep this principle in mind each day of our lives. Earnest effort, hard work—these things may sound ordinary, but it is ordinary words like these that contain the great truths of life.

Untangle Complex Problems to See Clearly

At Kyocera, employees and departments often argue sincerely and intensely about the best way to approach any given situation.

The subject of contention might be the delivery date of a new product or pricing. The production department will propose one solution, and the sales department will present an opposing opinion. When I was still president, many such controversies arose, and when the two involved parties could not come to an agreement, they frequently would bring the problem to me for my final judgment. After listening carefully to both sides, I would tell them my conclusion, and both parties invariably would be satisfied and return to their posts, their faces showing relief, as if they had never engaged in a heated argument.

They did not accept my final judgments merely because I happened to be the president. They did it because with no vested interest or ties, I was able to view the problem objectively. I could unravel the tangled threads of the problem to pinpoint its true cause and suggest a solution that was based on that understanding. When friction occurred between two departments, causing their relationship to grow complex and confusing, I often found that the root of the disagreement was something simple, trivial, and above all self-centered, such as one department's failure to consult with the appropriate person from the other department, or one department's failure to express appreciation for something the other department had done. After I had pinpointed the problem, I would return to the essence of what is right as a human being and be able to suggest a solution that satisfied all parties.

45

To make a fair and appropriate judgment, it is vital to have an unbiased perspective. From a neutral standpoint, the tangle of twigs and leaves will not distract us and we will be able to see the root of the problem clearly. We also will see that the majority of social problems, from major international conflicts to friction in the home, begin with the expectations and opinions of all involved parties. Each participant adds more reasons and arguments to create a strange and convoluted web. The more complicated a problem appears, the greater is the need to return to the starting line and follow simple principles when deciding the appropriate course of action. When we are confronted with a problem so difficult that we want to give up, the best approach is to assess what is right and what is wrong on the basis of an open mind and clear, simple principles.

The world-renowned mathematician Heisuke Hironaka, who serves as vice chairman of the Inamori Foundation, discovered a way to solve difficult mathematical propositions that no one had solved before. Instead of breaking problems down into factors, which is the common approach in both mathematics and science, he raises the dimensions of the equations. "A complex phenomenon," he pointed out, "is merely the projection of a simple fact." By looking at two-dimensional problems from a three-dimensional perspective, he was able to find clear and simple answers.

He uses a simple example to explain his process: "Imagine there's an intersection with no traffic light. Cars will converge from all four directions, resulting in a traffic jam and total chaos. Left as is, there is no way of solving this problem. That's because we're trying to solve it within a two-dimensional plane. But what happens if we add the factor of height, that is, a third dimension? To our flat, two-dimensional intersection we add another, higher level so that one road goes over the other and cars can go through the intersection without colliding. My approach to solving difficult mathematical problems is similar. In most cases, phenomena that appear complex are merely the projection of a simple structure. If we change our perspective, if we raise the dimension from which we view a problem, the answer will become clear to us."

As Hironaka pointed out, we need to view situations from a higher dimension, one that simplifies phenomena and extracts the essence of any given problem. This higher, three-dimensional perspective can be gained by possessing a fair, open, and unselfish mind that is detached from personal interests or self-serving motives.

Think Simply, Even about International Problems and Conflicts

Japanese war atrocities such as the Nanking massacre and sexual slavery have been a source of contention between China and Japan for many decades. I once attended a debate on whether Japan should apologize to China for its wartime atrocities. When I frankly said that I thought Japan should apologize, several university professors looked shocked. Apparently, not only is it extremely unusual for one country to apologize to another, it is frowned upon because it results in both loss of face and a legal disadvantage under international law for the apologizing country.

I can understand that personal feelings should be kept separate from national politics. However, it is a historical fact that Japan invaded China and behaved shamefully, and therefore I believe that the Japanese should apologize for the wrongs they committed. To apologize when you hurt someone is universally recognized as a righteous act. As such, asking forgiveness should transcend logic and common sense and take precedence over profit and honor. Apologizing when we're in the wrong is a simple unshakable principle, a standard that must be adhered to as a matter of course. To be true to that principle, we must apologize even if it means that we lose something.

A sincere and honest attitude cannot fail to touch the hearts of others. Although Japan has made an official apology for its wartime actions several times, China and Korea have yet to accept it. To me, this indicates that Japan's apology was insincere and politically motivated. It is also an excellent illustration of how we are all guilty of complicating life's simple problems.

We can find solutions to international disputes or economic conflicts if we return to their starting points. The more complex a problem appears to be, the more we need to address it with decisions and actions based on simple principles and pure concepts. This is the best way to get straight to the truth of any matter and avoid complicated projections and restrictive, biased perspectives.

Trade imbalances, for example, cause complex friction between countries, but the root cause of this problem is the existence of "national borders." Each country has its own independent policies and currency, and as a result, the balance of trade varies widely from country to country, with some countries enjoying healthy trade surpluses while others see a trade deficit year after year. With the globalization of the economy and the traffic of people and goods across borders, it has become clear that these separate national policies and currencies have become barriers that create economic disparity and friction. We would get closer to solving these international economic problems if we eliminated borders and unified government policies, if we treated the world as one country.

On the basis of this simple concept, I once proposed the formation of a federal world government in which the nations and peoples of the world would abolish national borders and form a single community that could develop in peace and harmony. To realize this goal we would need to establish an international organization to draw up and implement the new governing body's necessary policies. It's a bold idea that calls not only for a borderless economy but also for a borderless political system.

Of course, there are many issues that would need to be dealt with before this goal ever could be realized, but the creation of a federal world government is not mere idealism or an idle pipe dream. Developed nations already are being forced to align their economic policies with one another, and the authority of the state gradually is becoming more and more restricted. The birth of the European Union (EU) represents the forerunner of the type of federal world government that I envision. Through the EU, Europe has become a single community with integrated political and economic policies. The establishment of the euro as the common currency is a symbol of Europe's integration. Expanding this type of movement to the world is certainly not impossible.

Some people will claim that eliminating the nation-state will eliminate the distinct history and culture of each country. The elimination of nations, however, does not automatically mean that national cultures with their diverse histories will disappear. The human race has existed for much longer than the nation-state and will continue to exist far into the future. First there were people and then came the state, not the other way around. People may criticize my idea as unrealistically optimistic, but I believe we need to base our philosophy and our actions on a vision of the way human beings and the world should be.

49

Reason before Common Practice in International Negotiations

In this chapter, I have discussed the importance of following guiding principles in our thoughts and actions in all aspects of our lives. It also can be extremely effective to follow these guiding principles when we are dealing with people from other countries and negotiating with foreign companies. I have noticed that people from many Western nations have a firm philosophy concerning life and work, which enables them to compare their set of guiding principles with Japan's and debate the pros and cons of each.

When Kyocera was still a small, unknown firm, I actively approached many foreign companies to promote our products.

At the time, many Japanese companies were still introducing American technology into their workplaces, and I thought that recognition by American manufacturers would raise domestic demand for our products. Despite the fact that I spoke very little English, I decided to fly to the United States and meet with executives at companies I hoped would purchase Kyocera's products. The day before I left Japan for my first visit I remember going to a friend's house to learn how to use Western-style toilets, which were very rare in Japan. This was during the era when the exchange rate was 360 yen to the U.S. dollar and few Japanese traveled overseas.

I stayed in the United States for about a month and tried to sell Kyocera's products to one company after another without much success. More often than not I was turned away at the door before I had a chance to negotiate. In this strange land with its bewildering culture and customs, it looked like all I would get for my efforts was rejection and frustration. My desperation and the hardship of that visit remain a vivid memory. But I stuck with it, and as a result of perseverance and repeated negotiations, I began to see results and the number of deals Kyocera secured with foreign firms increased.

During my business trip to the United States, I noticed that in foreign countries and particularly in the United States people often used the word *reasonable* when considering a decision. Moreover, unlike Japan, the standard by which Americans judged reasonableness was not predicated on social custom or common practice but their own personal principles and value systems. They had a solid philosophy and criteria for judgment that were based on their beliefs. I found this extremely refreshing and stimulating.

The difference between the American understanding of reasonableness and Japan's, of course, arose from a fundamental difference in our cultures that is exemplified by the dissimilarity between the American and Japanese legal systems. Japanese law is based on the German model, which is basically statutory law. Legal decisions are made on the basis of legal text, and consequently the law can become quite dogmatic. The American system, in contrast, is based on precedent, which means that decisions are not as restricted by written statutes and can be adjusted to suit each individual case. There is a strong tendency in the American legal system for those involved to judge a case on the basis of personal good sense and decide if something is just or fair.

In countries that culturally value the concept of living one's life according to a personal philosophy, my approach of clearly identifying guiding principles is highly effective. I presented my sales arguments on the basis of my guiding principles during my negotiations for Kyocera, and if the other party agreed, it made a decision on the spot without any concern for company precedents or the size of the business. Thanks to this, I was able to conclude negotiations with foreign companies very quickly.

Globalization is progressing rapidly, and even an island country such as Japan must survive in an international society. In our work and in daily life we will need to interact and even argue with people from different countries. In Japanese culture, conflict is avoided and there is a tendency to pacify or give in to others when our opinions differ from theirs. North Americans and Europeans, however, come from a culture of logic, and therefore it is much more effective to state clearly and boldly what you think is reasonable and fair. They are quite capable of understanding and respecting such arguments.

Our criterion for judgment should always be what feels right as a human being. This standard is universal and transcends national boundaries. Even if cultural clashes occur, both parties

51

can understand and accept this universal principle. In the Kyo-cera company newsletter, an American manager with the Kyocera Group North American holding company in San Diego was quoted as saying something like the following:

> Culture differs depending on the nation or race. But in the end the philosophy for doing business and the basic principles for living are the same. For example, striving to achieve results in one's work and wanting to be of benefit to society are universal truths that can be found in every culture and religion.

He captured this concept perfectly. No matter where we work, we need a universal philosophy that serves as a standard for making business management decisions. The more universal the standard is, the more effective it will be and the more deeply it will be rooted in the ethical and moral concept of what is right as a human being. This concept is borderless. The guiding principles for life are shared by the entire human race and thus transcend national differences and the times in which we live.

CHAPTER 3

REFINE AND ELEVATE YOUR MIND

Losing the Beauty of the Japanese Soul

Japanese people seem to be forfeiting the very virtues that were once considered essential components of their culture. One such virtue is humility: the respect shown by bowing to others in greeting, the modesty to give credit to others instead of boasting of one's own triumphs, the humble attitude of letting others go before us. I know there are times in life when we have to assert ourselves, but I believe that forgetting the beauty of the Japanese soul, which is exemplified by humility, represents a great loss to the Japanese society and nation. It also makes Japan a less pleasant place to live.

Granted, it is almost impossible for ordinary people like me to maintain a humble attitude. Arrogance frequently rears its ugly head inside me. I developed many new technologies and products in the virgin field of fine ceramics and guided the remarkably speedy growth of Kyocera. Consequently, I receive a great deal of attention and praise. When I attend meetings, I am offered the best seat and often am asked for my opinion. Although I strive constantly to guard against my ego, sometimes a little voice in my mind tells me that all my efforts and achievements have granted me the right to be treated better than others. Then something suddenly will make me aware that I'm enjoying all the attention, and I am reminded to take myself to task for my lack of humility. I struggle with remaining humble often despite my training as a Buddhist priest.

Frankly, none of the talents I possess and none of the prestigious roles I have filled are necessarily uniquely mine. Someone else could have been born with my abilities or achieved what I have accomplished just as easily. All I did was strive to polish the gifts that were given to me.

I think that every talent we have has been entrusted to us; perhaps *loaned* is the more appropriate term. Whatever special abilities I may have and whatever achievements may result from these talents are mine, yet they do not belong solely to me. Our abilities and actions are not meant to be monopolized like private possessions; rather, they are meant to be used for others and for society. We should use them for the public good before using them for ourselves. When we use our talents for the benefit of others, I believe we are practicing the essence of humility.

As the spirit of humility has diminished in Japanese society, I have noticed a corresponding increase in the number of people who view their talents as their personal property. This trend is especially evident among people in positions of leadership who ought to be setting a good example. Major companies with long traditions and impressive achievements recently have been plagued by scandals, indicating a weakening of their guiding precepts and ethical compass. Similarly, certain public officials have been exploiting their authority to line their pockets despite the fact that they are paid from our taxes to represent us. The fact that these politicians use their abilities for corrupt purposes suggests that they believe their talents are their own. Failing to recognize their talents as a trust from heaven, they use their abilities to satisfy their selfish desires rather than to benefit others.

A Leader Needs Virtue before Talent

When one looks at those in positions of power who behave unethically through the lens of my formula for living, attitude × effort × ability, it is clear that these individuals have considerable ability. They also have enthusiasm and work much harder than the average person does, but their attitude has led them to use their gifts in the wrong way. In the end, their criminal behavior harms not only society but themselves.

Our attitude is our approach to living, our philosophy or ethical view of life, and it is a window to our character, which encompasses our attitude and virtues such as humility. If our character is twisted or evil, no matter how much ability and enthusiasm we may have—in fact, the more of those qualities that we have—the greater the negative value of our results.

I think the problem with Japanese leaders is rooted more in the way the Japanese people choose them than in the actual individuals themselves. We consistently select leaders on the basis of resourcefulness and ability, not character, and tend to measure their ability by academic performance alone. A typical example is the appointment of people who excel on public servant examinations to important government posts and elite career tracks.

The Japanese approach to choosing leaders is directly related to Japan's postwar emphasis on economic growth. Since the war's close, people have begun to value traits and practical skills that directly contribute to tangible results over character, which is

55

harder to define. The strongly rooted Japanese custom of electing politicians who give kickbacks to their home districts demonstrates that many people prefer leaders with ability even if those leaders lack virtue. It is hard to break free from this mentality.

In the past, however, I think the Japanese people had a broader perspective. Takamori Saigo (1827–1877), a statesman in nineteenth-century Japan, once said, "To men of high virtue, give high office; to men of many achievements, give cash." In other words, achievement can be rewarded with money, but high leadership positions should be given to people of noble character. Although over a century has passed since Takamori spoke these words, far from becoming outdated, his remarks contain a universal philosophy that has withstood the test of time. Now more than ever, when the moral fabric of contemporary society is disintegrating, we should take Takamori's words to heart.

Leaders should be judged by their characters rather than by their abilities. People with extraordinary abilities need the self-control to avoid sinking into pride or using their talents in the wrong way. This is virtue; this is character. Some think the term *virtue* is outdated, but there is nothing either old or new about cultivating character. Lu Kun (1536–1618), a Chinese scholar-official in the late Ming dynasty, writes on the universality of virtue in a work called *Shen Yin Yu*. According to Kun, the first qualification for leadership is depth, the second is generous courage, and the third is sagacious eloquence. These qualities also can be interpreted as character, courage, and ability. All three attributes are important, but if I were to prioritize them, character would rank first, courage second, and ability third.

Practice Daily Reflection and Refine Your Character

Since the end of World War II, Japan has had many leaders with the third qualification—ability. Important government posts have gone to eloquent speakers with exceptional ability and plenty of practical knowledge. In contrast, people with good characters, although they may not have been looked down upon, have been relegated to the wings. Japan has installed leaders who lack inner ethical standards as well as depth of character and thus are unsuited to leadership. Poor leadership, I believe, is one cause of Japan's recent government and business scandals and the root of the moral decay that is infesting Japanese society.

Leaders of scandal-tainted organizations who are interviewed on television rarely exhibit any depth of character when they are called to task for their actions. Instead, they mouth apologetic phrases from a prepared script: "We should never have done it. We'll make sure it doesn't happen again." Their words sound superficial and insincere. Their confusion and their desire to gloss over their mistakes and evade responsibility are clearly evident, but they sadly lack a willingness to confront the problem, accept responsibility, offer an honest explanation, or rectify their mistakes. I can only conclude that these so-called leaders have no guiding philosophy, no standard to distinguish good from evil or right from wrong. If that is how our leaders are choosing to behave, it is not surprising that children have lost their respect for adults.

More than ability or eloquence, leaders need depth of character. They must be humble, introspective, and disciplined; they must have the courage to defend justice and the love to continually refine their souls. They must strive constantly to do what is right as human beings. Ancient Chinese texts urge us to forgo the four troubles: deceit, egotism, self-indulgence, and arrogant pride, and if we aspire to be leaders, we must strive to follow this noble way of life. In other words, aspiring leaders must demonstrate noblesse oblige.

Some may scoff and say that the idea of doing what is right as a human being is childish and suited only for an elementary school morality class. But it is precisely because adults have failed to practice the moral precepts they learned in grade school that society's values have been severely shaken and people's souls have been desolated. How many adults today can confidently teach their children moral values? How many people can present a clear standard or explain ethical principles? How many people can distinguish right from wrong and have the necessary spirit and depth of character to do so? How can we feel anything but ashamed when we look at what we have become?

It isn't hard to know the right thing to do. We just need to reflect on the simple moral guidelines we learned as children—be honest, don't lie or cheat, don't be greedy—reexamine their meanings, and put them into practice.

Six *Shojin* for Refining the Soul

Of course, it is not only leaders who need to refine and elevate their souls. Every one of us should be working hard to become not just intelligent and capable but also, and most important, righteous. The elevation of the soul is the purpose, the meaning of our lives. Life is nothing other than the process of refining our true nature as human beings.

What does it mean to elevate our souls? Far from being a complicated process for attaining a state of enlightenment or supreme goodness, it simply means striving to make our souls a little more beautiful, a little more advanced, than they were when we were born. As we do this, we learn to control our egos; gain tranquillity, kindness, and consideration for others; and develop an unselfish mind. This process of transforming and beautifying our souls is the ultimate purpose of life.

From the perspective of the universe, our lives constitute nothing more than a fleeting second. This is precisely why we should strive to increase the value of our lives before the final curtain call, as it is within this process that we find both our nobility and the essence of life. We struggle through our temporal existence, which we live only once, experiencing pain, suffering, and anxiety as well as joy and happiness. These experiences—this process—become the grit with which we refine our souls to make them a little nobler each day. If we can accomplish this, our lives will have been well worth living.

Just as there are infinite routes to the top of a mountain, there are many methods for and approaches to refining our souls. From my own experience, I have found that the following six *shojin* (diligent efforts) can aid us immensely in elevating our souls, and I share them with you here as a guide.

1. Work harder than anyone else, study harder than anyone else, and carry on single-mindedly. If you have enough time to complain, you have enough time to improve yourself, even if only a little.

2. Be humble, not proud. A Chinese proverb warns us that "only the humble will find fortune." Humility attracts happiness and purifies the soul.

3. Reflect every day. Assess your actions and state of mind daily to see if you are thinking only of yourself, if you are being mean or cowardly. Exercise self-control and self-reflection and strive to correct your behavior.

4. Be thankful that you are alive. Believe that you are lucky just to be living and train your heart to be grateful for even the smallest thing.

5. Fill your days with good deeds and selfless conduct. As the Japanese proverb says, "The home that accumulates good deeds will be blessed with unexpected fortune." Do good

things, be of service to others, and strive to be considerate in word and deed. Those who accumulate good deeds will receive a good reward.

6. Don't complain or dwell on the negative. Maintain a tranquil mind at all times. Don't worry about the things over which you have no control. It is important to do your very best so that you have no regrets.

I constantly strive to remember and practice these six *shojin*. They may seem rather ordinary on paper, but it is important to incorporate them slowly but surely into our daily lives. They are meant to be practiced, not just written down, framed, and hung on the wall.

Learning Gratitude from the *Kakure Nenbutsu*

In this age of material prosperity, the poverty and emptiness of our souls are increasingly evident. The spirit of gratitude, which is one of the six *shojin* mentioned above, seems particularly lacking today. In a world inundated with material wealth, this is the time to return to contentment and gratitude.

When I was young and Japan was still a poor country, the value that I held most dear, the virtue to which I most aspired, was sincerity. I strove to be sincere in my life and work, to live fully and earnestly without cutting corners. At the time, sincerity was inherent in the Japanese people, one of their distinguishing virtues. Japan's poverty was followed by rapid economic growth, and as Japanese society became more affluent and Kyocera prospered, gratitude began to occupy a larger space within my heart. I could not help feeling immensely thankful for all the blessings I received through sincere hard work. My sense of gratitude grew strong and sturdy until it became a virtue that I practiced in my daily life. When I look back over my life, I can see how thankfulness has flowed like an underground current through my moral values. I also can see how it is rooted in an experience from my childhood.

My family home is in Kagoshima at the southern tip of the southernmost of Japan's four main islands. When I was four or five my father took me with him to participate in a secret Buddhist service known as the *kakure nenbutsu*. This custom had been preserved secretly by faithful adherents of a Buddhist sect that had been suppressed for centuries and it was still practiced by followers of this sect when I was a child.

Together with other parents and children my father and I climbed a steep mountain path through the darkness, lighting our way with lanterns. Silence prevailed, and as I trotted along after my father, I remember being filled with mystical reverence. Our destination was a humble dwelling inside which a Buddhist priest chanted sutras before an altar set inside a closet. Only a few candles lit the room, and when we sat down, we melted into the darkness. The children who had made the pilgrimage were made to kneel behind the priest and listen to him chant in his quiet, deep voice. When he had finished, we were instructed to offer incense and pray before the altar one by one. As we did so, the priest spoke to each of us in turn. He told many of the children to come again, but to me he said, "You don't need to come back. You are finished. From now on, every day give thanks to the Buddha. Every day say, '*Nanman, nanman, arigato*' [I trust in the Buddha of Immeasurable Light. Thank you.]." Then he turned to my father and told him that he did not need to bring me to the hidden Buddha again. Although only a little boy, I felt as though I had just passed a test or received special recognition, and I was proud and pleased.

My encounter in that spiritual dwelling made a deep impression on me. It was my first religious experience, and from it, I learned the importance of gratitude, which has shaped my heart and mind. Even now the phrase of thanksgiving that the

61

priest imparted to me often runs through my head or rises unconsciously to my lips. When I visited the great cathedrals of Europe, I was so moved by their majesty that I chanted these words spontaneously. *Nanman, nanman, arigato* is a prayer that transcends any religion or sect, and it has become a part of my innermost being.

Be Ready to Express Appreciation in Every Situation

The prayer I learned on my pilgrimage, which even a child can remember, became the model for my faith and nurtured my spirit of gratitude. Reciting its words during good times or bad, for anyone and anything, fostered my spirit of gratitude and encouraged me to do what was right.

Fortune and misfortune are like strands of the same rope; braided together they make up our lives. Therefore, we should always be grateful whether our luck is good or bad, whether it is sunny or cloudy. We should remember to be thankful not only when fortune smiles upon us but also when we are faced with difficulties. Just being alive is something to be grateful for. Gratitude elevates the mind and is the first step toward creating a brighter future.

Of course, being grateful during difficulties is easier said than done. It's next to impossible for someone to always be thankful, rain or shine, and it is especially difficult to welcome adversity as a test. We are much more likely to protest against the unfairness of fate and feel resentful of our hardships. That is human nature. We also do not automatically feel grateful when we are blessed with good fortune. In fact, we often take our blessings for granted or even greedily ask for more. Again, that is human nature. We forget the spirit of gratitude, and consequently happiness eludes us.

We need to consciously program our rational minds to be grateful. When gratitude does not spring up naturally inside us, we need to impose it on our minds and prepare ourselves at all times to say, "Thank you." We must constantly and consciously prepare our hearts to be open receptacles for gratitude, to see tests and difficulties as opportunities to help us grow, to see good fortune as a gift that we must not waste.

Gratitude arises from the state of contentment, not from discontent or lack of fulfillment. But what is contentment? Does contentment come from having plenty, and discontent from not having enough? On a material level, the answer is yes, but what satisfies one person may not satisfy another. Some people feel content with very little, whereas others always want more no matter how much they already have. Some people never stop complaining, whereas others are able to maintain a state of contentment no matter what their situation is. Obviously, gratitude depends on our state of mind and not on our material circumstances. No matter what our material situation is, if we are thankful, we can find contentment.

Have an Open Mind and a Joyous Heart

63

Just as a spirit of gratitude brings joy into our lives, an open mind inspires progress in our lives. Open-mindedness entails listening openly to criticism even when you don't want to hear it and appropriately correcting your actions now rather than later. When we open our minds to others, we nurture our abilities and hone our spirits.

Konosuke Matsushita frequently spoke about the importance of having an open mind. He had little education, and to grow and improve himself, Matsushita strove to learn as much as he could from others. He retained a sense of open-minded learning throughout his life. Even after he was deified as the "god of management," Matsushita never forgot that he was still a student. Therein lay his true greatness.

Of course, having an open mind does not mean doing exactly what everyone tells you to do. Rather, it means recognizing your inadequacies and, with the humility this knowledge inspires, sparing no effort to improve. To be truly open-minded, you must develop and constantly apply to your life the ability to hear others' opinions and to see yourself honestly.

Early in my career as an engineer, I always shouted with glee and jumped up and down when my hard work produced the results I had hoped for. My assistant, however, disapproved of my behavior. One day, I asked him why he didn't get excited, too. He gave me a sharp look and said bluntly, "How can you be so childish? You get so excited about trivial things. Something worthy of so much excitement only happens once or twice in a lifetime. You make yourself look so shallow doing that."

His words hit me like a bucket of cold water, but I rallied and said, "You know, you're probably right, but I still think that it's better to be sincerely and simply happy when you see results, no matter how small they may be. It may seem shallow to you, but it's this joy and gratitude that gives me the energy to carry on with my research."

Although my response came from off the top of my head, what I said to my assistant clearly reflected my approach to life, my philosophy for living. I was trying to convey to him the importance of acknowledging even the most trivial events in our lives with a spirit of joy and gratitude that remains untainted by logical argument.

The habit of daily reflection, which is crucial to refining a person's character, is actually the product of maintaining an open mind. No matter how hard we try to be humble, it is easy to revert to acting as if we know everything. Opportunities for self-reflection help us recognize our faults such as arrogance, pride, conceit, and carelessness and reinforce our guiding principles and self-discipline. Eventually, if we get into the habit of faithfully practicing daily self-reflection, we will be able to elevate our minds.

When I take time to reflect, I often find myself saying, "God, forgive me." If I notice myself boasting or being insincere, I'll go home and ask God to forgive my negative attitude and promise that I'll try to avoid these actions in the future. I wait until I'm alone to address God in this way because I apologize so loudly that anyone overhearing me might think I had gone crazy. With an open heart and mind I voice the words that come through reflection and resolve to try again the next day to be a humble student of life.

"God, forgive me" and *"Nanman, nanman, arigato"* are my favorite phrases. Both expressions capture the spirit of gratitude and self-reflection in clear but simple words and form the guiding principles for directing my conduct along the right path.

A Buddhist Tale of Human Greed

In addition to thankfulness and open-minded self-reflection, we need to become detached from excessive desire if we wish to refine our characters. Greed, however, is rooted deeply in the human heart, a poison that eats away at our souls and causes us to choose the wrong path in life. The Buddha told the following tale to illustrate how easily human nature is ensnared by greed.

One day a traveler hurried home against a chilly wind in the late autumn. As he walked, he suddenly noticed white objects strewn along the path. Bending closer, he realized that they were human bones. Why, he wondered, are there bones along the path? It was strange and uncanny, but he was in a hurry to get home, and so the traveler continued on his way. Just then, a huge tiger appeared ahead, roaring thunderously. The traveler stopped in shock. Now he knew where the bones had come from. They were the remains of poor travelers who had been consumed by the tiger.

The traveler hastily turned and fled back along the path, but somehow he lost his way and found himself at the edge of a precipice. Below him surged the roiling sea, and behind him stalked the tiger. Unable to go forward or backward, he began to climb a single pine tree that grew at the edge of the cliff. But the tiger also began to climb, digging its fearsomely long claws into the tree.

Thinking that this would be the end, the traveler began preparing to die when suddenly he noticed a wisteria vine dangling from the branch in front of him. He grabbed the vine and used it to slide down the cliff but it was not long enough to reach the ground and he was left dangling in midair. At the edge of the cliff, the tiger glared down at him, licking its lips. Below him, three dragons, one red, one black, and one blue, gathered in the raging sea, waiting to eat him if he fell. Worse still, he heard a munching noise and looked up to find a black mouse and a white mouse taking turns chewing on the vine that he was grasping. If the mice continued nibbling, they would gnaw right through the vine, and he would plunge straight into the mouths of the waiting dragons.

There was no escape and nowhere to turn. Desperately, the traveler jerked at the vine to ward off the mice. As he did that, a drop of liquid fell onto his cheek. It was honey. There was a beehive at the root of the vine, and every time he shook his lifeline, honey dripped into his mouth. Captivated by its sweetness, the traveler forgot the danger he was in. He forgot that he was trapped between the tiger and the dragons. He forgot that the mice were chewing away at his only salvation. All he thought about was shaking the vine to get more honey.

This, the Buddha teaches us, is the nature of a human being enmeshed in desire. Though driven into a desperately dangerous corner, he can focus on nothing but sweet honey. The Russian author Leo Tolstoy reportedly said that no other story captures the essence of human nature as well as the one you just read.

I agree. The Buddha's tale deftly depicts our way of life and portrays how deep-rooted human desire is.

At the same time, the Buddha's story is allegorical. The tiger represents death or illness; the pine tree, status, wealth, and fame; and the white and black mice, night and day, the passage of time. We live in constant fear of death and seek to escape it, clinging to life, yet our grasp on that single vine is very frail. The vine will wear away with the passage of time, and each passing day and year only brings us closer to death. However, we still want the honey—our desires—even if its procurement shortens our lives. Our true nature, as the Buddha shows us through this story, is found in our inability to detach ourselves from our wretched desires.

Detaching Ourselves from the Three Poisons

The honey in the Buddha's story represents the various pleasures that gratify our desires. Similarly, the dragons represent human desires and selfish thoughts. The red dragon is a broker for anger, the black dragon for greed, and the blue dragon for envy. In Buddhism anger, greed, and envy are called the three poisons. The Buddha warns us that the three poisons will lead to our downfall, as they are the cause of the 108 worldly desires that torment humankind. They are toxic and twist around our hearts so that we cannot escape.

We certainly seem to spend the majority of our days caught up in anger, greed, and envy. We want to get ahead of others and have a better lifestyle than they do, so we become beholden to the desire for fame and fortune, which lies concealed in every heart. When this desire is thwarted, we feel angry and frustrated, and these negative feelings consequently turn into envy of those who have the things we want. The majority of us are constantly caught up in this vicious cycle of desire.

In that respect, we are no better than a child or infant. When I show attention to one of my grandchildren in the presence of another grandchild, the other grandchild immediately becomes jealous. Clearly, the poison of envy already taints our hearts when we are only two or three years old. Of course, desire and ambition cannot be totally condemned from our lives. We need them to some extent because they give us energy for living, but we should be aware that our desires can become toxic poisons and cause us endless suffering. It is ironic that the energy we need to exist can destroy our happiness.

Because our desires can take the joy from our lives, it is important to detach ourselves from worldly desires as much as possible. We may not be able to eradicate the three poisons from our lives completely, but we can strive to control them by diligently practicing the simple guidelines of sincerity, gratitude, and self-reflection discussed so far. There is no shortcut.

It is also important to develop the habit of making rational judgments in our daily lives. Every day we are forced to make decisions. If we make decisions on the spur of the moment, more often than not they will be based on instinct, in other words, on self-interest. Instead of responding immediately, we should put our first spontaneous judgment on hold, take a deep breath, and ask ourselves whether our decision is based on selfish desires. Putting this cushion of time between our thoughts and our actions allows us to make a judgment that is based on reason. Building this rational circuit within our thought processes is an important step in detaching ourselves from desire.

To suppress selfish desires is to develop a pure and altruistic mind. I believe that putting others before oneself is the highest human virtue. Once we develop an attitude of selflessness and consideration for others, of dedicating our lives to service, we no longer will be troubled by worldly desires, our hearts will be cleansed of poison, and our desires will be pure.

The Sword of Righteousness Leads to Success

Chapter 4 deals with the subject of an altruistic mind in more detail, but let me reiterate that the pure, unselfish desire to contribute to the world and to others will always be fulfilled. Because it is the highest desire we can have, altruism will always produce the best results in our lives. Conversely, desires that are clouded by self-interest may be realized at first, but that success is only temporary because, in the words of Koichi Tsukamoto, such desires unsheathe the "sword of evil."

Koichi Tsukamoto (1920–1998) was the founder of Wacoal, a worldwide lingerie and apparel company. He and I moved in the same business circles in Kyoto, and I came to know him very well. Tsukamoto had lived through the Battle of Imphal in northeastern India. Launched by Japanese commanders toward the end of World War II with the objective of destroying Allied troops and invading India, the plan failed and the Japanese were driven back into Burma with devastating losses. Among the 55 members of Tsukamoto's platoon, only 3 survived.

During the postwar chaos in Japan, Tsukamoto started peddling fashion accessories and went on to build a successful business. His narrow escape from death convinced him that God was on his side, and therefore he was certain he could realize any business venture he attempted. One day, however, his most trusted assistant, the company vice president, told him, "You're right that God is on your side—but not when you unsheathe the sword of evil. You have two swords: the sword of righteousness and the sword of evil. When you use the first sword, you succeed in everything you do. But when you use the other, nothing goes right. That shows that God is with you because he helps you when you use the sword of righteousness but he turns away from you when you use the sword of evil."

Tsukamoto was struck by his assistant's keen observation, and so was I when he told me. The sword of evil represents impure and selfish desires, thoughts that are tainted with self-interest, a solo performance concerned only with personal gain. Precisely because these selfish desires are so powerful, success cannot last long. In contrast, when our desire is pure and unselfish and we strive to achieve it with heart and soul, we can achieve long-term success.

Granted, there are times when we diligently strive to reach a goal but nothing seems to work out. Yet it is often when we are at our wits' end that we receive an inspiration or a sudden revelation from the most unexpected source that shows us what to do. In these revelatory moments, it feels just as if the creator of the universe were giving us a gentle shove from behind. There is a Japanese saying, "None can escape the net of heaven." Although it may seem that God isn't paying attention, he is watching very carefully, distinguishing right from wrong. Therefore, if we want lasting success, our vision and aspirations must be pure. We first must desire with a pure heart, free from self, and then we must unsheathe the sword of righteousness. Only then can we accomplish our goals and prosper.

Work Brings the Greatest Joy of All

Another essential factor in refining our souls and elevating our characters is diligence. It is through hard work and dedicated efforts that we prosper spiritually and gain depth of character.

I believe it is through our work that we truly can experience joy. I'm sure some will claim that single-minded devotion to one's job makes for a boring life and insist that we need time to relax and pursue other interests. What they don't realize, however, is that we are able to enjoy other interests precisely because our work is fulfilling. If our hearts are not in our work, we may enjoy other things briefly but never taste the true joy that springs naturally from the heart.

The joy of working is not akin to the instantaneous gratification one gets from popping a candy in one's mouth. As the old maxim says, the roots of labor are bitter but the fruits are sweet. Joy wells up inside of us as we work our way through difficulties and tests; it is waiting for us when we transcend the trials involved with hardship. There's tremendous satisfaction in overcoming tests and doing one's best, which is why the joy we gain through hard work is so different from the joy we experience when we have fun. There is no greater joy than the joy of working. For most of us, work accounts for the majority of our lives. If we can't find fulfillment in our work, no matter how hard we try to find joy elsewhere, we will always feel that something is missing.

Working diligently does much more than fulfill us. It also builds and refines our character and helps us hone our philosophy for living. In the practice of Zen Buddhism, itinerant priests carry out all the monastery's daily chores, from preparing the meals to sweeping the yard. For the priests, these tasks are another form of practicing meditation: There is essentially no difference between devoting oneself to the daily chores of life and achieving a state of spiritual oneness by sitting in meditation. According to Buddhism, daily chores are a spiritual practice and working diligently is a road that leads to enlightenment.

Enlightenment means elevating your soul. It is the highest and ultimate spiritual state you achieve as you work to refine your soul. The Buddha taught us the *Rokuharamitsu*, the perfection of the six virtues, as a means for reaching enlightenment.

Remember the Six Perfections

The *Rokuharamitsu* helps us move a little closer to the state of enlightenment in the path of the Buddha by offering these six essential practices for refining our minds and elevating our souls:

71

1. *Fuse*: This is the act of selfless giving. It means thinking of others before oneself and consciously focusing on being kind to others. Although the term is used commonly in Japan to refer to almsgiving, *fuse* originally meant serving all people selflessly even in the face of personal sacrifice and, when that isn't possible, striving to develop a generous and sympathetic heart. We can elevate our souls by possessing a heart full of love for others.

2. *Jikai*: Also known as observance of the Buddhist precepts, *jikai* is the avoidance of wrongdoing. As human beings, we harbor many worldly desires. We already have seen that greed, discontent, and anger are three spiritual poisons that are very difficult to eliminate; therefore, we must strive to control our selfish desires and align our speech and actions with righteousness. To control worldly desires such as greed, indulgence, doubt, and envy is to practice *jikai*.

3. *Shojin*: To practice *shojin* is to make a diligent effort in whatever one does. I see this essential practice as the spirit of trying harder than anyone else. The lives of great people such as Ninomiya Sontoku, the uneducated peasant that was introduced in the Prologue, are excellent examples of how diligent effort elevates the mind and refines character.

4. *Ninniku*: The practice of patience in adversity is *ninniku*. Life is full of ups and downs, and we encounter many difficulties during our short existence. To practice patience is to strive even when the going is rough. It is to never allow adversity to crush us and to never try to avoid it either. Patience in hardship makes one's spirit strong and refines one's character.

5. *Zenjo*: In this turbulent, busy society, we are always hurrying toward the future and rarely have time to think

deeply. For this reason, we need to stop at least once a day to calm the turmoil in our minds and look quietly at ourselves, concentrating and focusing our minds on a single point. It is not necessary to engage in formal meditation. Just find a moment in your busy schedule to quiet your mind. When you take time for thought, you are practicing *zenjo*.

6. *Chie*: By practicing the five virtues previously described, we can receive *chie*, the eternal truth of the universe, and attain a state of enlightenment. At the moment of enlightenment, we can approach the great truth that moves all nature and controls the universe—we can draw nearer to the *chie* of which the Buddha speaks.

Refining the Mind through Daily Work

The six essential practices of the *Rokuharamitsu* show us the path we must travel to reach enlightenment. Among all of the practices, *shojin*, diligent effort, is the easiest to follow in our daily lives, and its application is the most basic and important way to improve our characters. The key to life is to strive steadily and continuously and never give up, to do our best at whatever role or job has been given to us, whether at work, at home, or at school. The path to refining one's character, elevating one's mind, and attaining enlightenment thus can be found in one's daily work.

I am strongly attracted to people who have devoted their entire lives to one field, such as the master carpenters who use traditional techniques to design and build Japanese shrines. They have mastered their skills and refined their character through long and unceasing effort. Their outstanding ability, the unshakable philosophy they have acquired through their work, the depth of their character, and the keenness of their insight all strike a chord in my heart. When a carpenter who has concentrated his life in one field reaches the age of 75 or 85, the weight of his character and the power of his presence are palpable. The words he speaks, which are often few and far between, seem almost mystical: "The wood has life." "The tree speaks to me."

Such men appear far nobler than any great philosopher or religious leader. They begrudge no effort and suffer repeated trials and hardships in their single-minded quest to master their trade. There is something awe-inspiring in the depths their characters achieve and the heights their minds reach through this diligent effort (*shojin*). These men make me aware yet again of just how noble an act working is. Their *shojin* reminds me that enlightenment can indeed be found in daily work.

Shojin can be practiced not only by craftsmen but by athletes as well. The major league baseball player Ichiro Suzuki (1973–) reached his level of expertise through the practice of *shojin*. Ichiro dreamed of becoming a major leaguer from childhood and practiced batting every day without fail. At an age when most children would be out playing, he had a goal and worked diligently toward it. When he was in high school, Ichiro reportedly said, "If you tell me to get a hit, I can." This was not arrogance on his part; he actually had become that skilled at hitting through hard work and dedication. In Ichiro today we can see the results of *shojin*.

No one has ever mastered any profession without steady, diligent effort. Only through loving our work and striving to be the best do we learn the meaning and value of life, refine our minds, shape our characters, and master the truth of life.

The Meaning of Work; Regaining Pride in Diligence

At the beginning of this chapter I mentioned that Japanese society needs to regain its humility. I think that diligence is yet another virtue Japan needs to retrieve.

In modern times and particularly since the end of World War II, the meaning and value of work have been interpreted in excessively materialistic terms. Japanese society has accepted material prosperity as a person's ultimate goal and believes that a job is merely a means of receiving money in exchange for one's time. The perception that work is just a way to make a living naturally has led to the view that we should try to make as much money as possible with as little effort as possible. This notion has spread throughout Japan and even permeates its schools.

Educators are deeply involved in building children's characters during their formative years, providing them with guidance and support. Teaching thus transcends the realm of ordinary work. It is a noble profession, a sacred vocation that requires its practitioners to teach by example. But teachers today seem to have lost their integrity. They have abandoned pride in their profession, insisting instead that they are mere laborers who sell by the hour the time they spend imparting knowledge to students. The actions and attitudes of Japan's teachers are indirect causes of the decline in the country's educational system, whose problems include the breakdown of classroom discipline.

Japan was not always this way. The Japanese people retained the spirit of diligence right through the period of phenomenal economic growth that lasted until the early 1970s. But when Westerners began to criticize the Japanese for working too hard, the government and the private sector scrambled to decrease the Japanese people's average number of working hours and increase their leisure time. As a result, enthusiastic dedication to one's work began to be seen almost as a crime. Japan let this change in attitude slip by virtually unnoticed, and people no longer value work as much as they used to.

I do not mean to condemn the Western approach to life, which sees leisure as the source of tranquillity and composure. I think it was a big mistake, however, for Japan to dismiss the value of hard work and introduce the concept of leisure as a means to serenity without first critically assessing its potential effect on Japanese culture. The Japanese people made another mistake when they began viewing work only as the material means for making a living. As I mentioned earlier, work plays a significant role in refining one's soul and honing one's character. It was not long ago that Japan and other Asian countries fully appreciated this spiritual aspect of work, regarding it as a means to building character and humanity.

General Douglas MacArthur, who led the American occupation government in Japan, testified before Congress about the Japanese work ethic in his policy discussions for the Far East. He declared that Japan's labor force was superior in terms of both quality and quantity than that of any other country, noting that Japanese workers had a deep respect for work and an understanding that happiness is found more often in work than it is in leisure.

In the past, the Japanese people found profound meaning and value in work. They were well aware that diligent effort gave value and meaning to their lives and enriched their hearts, and they saw their work as their reason for being. They had the spirituality to take joy in work over leisure, the ability to make even tedious tasks enjoyable through innovation, and the wisdom to take responsibility for their work as a personal and not imposed choice.

Today, when we have all but lost sight of the value of work, it is time to reassess its significance. People grow through their work. By dedicating themselves to their jobs, they elevate their minds and enrich their souls and in the end make their lives that much better.

CHAPTER 4

LIVE WITH AN ATTITUDE OF SELFLESS SERVICE

Encountering Compassion

In September 1997 I took the name Daiwa and became a lay priest at Enpukuji Temple in Kyoto. I had intended to begin my training in June but was diagnosed with stomach cancer just before my start date and had to undergo surgery. On September 7, a little over two months after the operation, I began training alongside the regular priests while continuing to live in the secular world.

Two months later I moved to the priests' temple for a short period to undertake ascetic practice. As I still was recovering from my operation, I found the training quite rigorous, but through it I gained an experience I will never forget. Early in the winter, the priests and I committed ourselves to the practice of *takuhatsu*: begging for alms. Wearing a simple cotton garment, sandals of braided straw, and a straw hat over my shaved head, I stood with the other priests at the doorway of people's homes and chanted prayers. *Takuhatsu* was physically very strenuous for someone like me who was unaccustomed to it. My toes, which stuck out over the edge of my sandals, soon were rubbed raw by the pavement, and after only half a day of walking my body felt like an old dishrag.

However, I continued traveling door to door for hours, following the other priests. Finally, at dusk we headed home, and I dragged my aching body back to the temple. On our way the priests and I passed by a park where an elderly woman in coveralls was sweeping. When she caught sight of us, she hurried over, still clutching her broom, and slipped 500 yen into my satchel as if it were the most natural thing to do.

I have never felt such deep emotion or such indescribable bliss as I did at that moment. Without hesitation or any trace of condescension, this woman, who surely was not well off, gave 500 yen to a mere priest in training. The beauty of her spirit was purer and more refreshing than anything I had experienced in my 65 years of life. Through her spontaneous act of compassion I felt touched by divine love. Although very simple, her act was the manifestation of the ultimate human attribute: warmhearted kindness and an ability to put others first. Her spontaneous good deed taught me the essence of altruism.

Altruism in Buddhist terms is compassion; in Christianity, it is called love. To be altruistic simply means dedicating oneself to the service of others and the world. I believe altruism is an indispensable key to living and, for businessmen like me, to running a company. This concept may sound grandiose, but it is actually perfectly rational. Service to others begins with the consideration we give to the people around us: wanting to feed your children good food, wanting to make your spouse smile, wanting to make your parents comfortable after all the worry you caused them when you were growing up. Working so that you can support your family, helping a friend, caring for your parents—these simple acts in the end will contribute to society, the nation, and the world. In that sense, the altruistic act of the woman who handed me alms can be seen as equivalent to the actions of Mother Teresa.

Human beings are born with the desire to serve others and the world. When I hear about the many young people who volunteer their services in areas devastated by natural disasters, I am convinced that altruism is a natural response of the human soul. I am sure many people will agree that we feel the deepest, purest happiness not when we satisfy our egos but when we give to others. Wise people know that when we dedicate ourselves to serving others, we also benefit.

Your Attitude Can Change Hell into Paradise

More than 40 years ago, when Kyocera was still a small company, I told new employees, "Your parents and many other people have helped you get this far in life. Now that you've joined the workforce, it's your turn to contribute. As an adult, you should no longer seek to receive but to give. You must change your viewpoint 180 degrees."

I communicated this message to my new employees because Kyocera was still too small a company to be able to extend adequate social benefits to its workers. Previously, university graduates who had entered our company had complained because they had expected better working conditions than Kyocera was able to offer them. It didn't take me long to realize that people who are dependent on others are always complaining about what they don't have. In response, I told our new employees, "It's true this is a small company and we don't have a proper system or facilities in place yet. But you are the ones who will help this company grow and develop so that in the future we can provide proper benefits."

My words were intended to help my employees see that as initiates of adult society, they needed to completely shift their perspectives and start giving to others. At the time I did not know the word *altruism* or have a solid philosophy concerning it, but even so I continued to teach Kyocera's young employees about the importance of continually striving to be of service, in whatever small way, to others.

When I entered the priesthood at Enpukuji, a wise priest told me a story that illustrates how important it is to think of others before oneself, to serve others even if doing so entails personal sacrifice.

"I've heard that in the next world there is a heaven and a hell," a young Buddhist priest once said to a senior priest. "What is hell like?"

"Well, it's true there's a heaven and a hell," the senior priest answered. "But there isn't really much difference between the two. On the surface, they look much the same. The only difference is the hearts of those who live there." The elder priest went on to explain that in both heaven and hell there is a large cooking pot filled with delicious noodles, but the only utensils provided for eating them are yardlong chopsticks. The inmates of hell all plunge their chopsticks into the pot at once, thinking only of sating their own hunger, and although they manage to grasp the noodles, the chopsticks are too long to bring to their mouths. Frustrated, they try to grab food from one another, and the noodles go flying everywhere. In the end, they starve, tormented by the sight of all that delicious food.

In heaven the conditions are exactly the same, but everyone picks up the noodles with his or her chopsticks and offers them to the person sitting on the opposite side of the table, saying, "Here, you eat first." The other person accepts the food and says, "Thank you, and let me return your kindness." Their hearts are content.

The wise priest's story illustrates the fact that although we all live in the same world, our experience of it as heaven or as hell depends on whether we feel warmth and compassion for others. It is for this reason that I repeatedly tell my employees that they need to develop an altruistic mind. Good business requires that our hearts be filled with consideration for others and for the world.

Benefiting Others Is the Starting Point of Business

In today's business world, where survival of the fittest rules, people often suspect that I have ulterior motives when I discuss the importance of altruism, love, and caring for others. But I am not interested in manipulating words to gain some objective. I am only trying to convey what I believe and put it into practice.

History shows that capitalism arose from Christian civilizations, particularly from Puritan ethics. According to the German political scientist and sociologist Max Weber (1864–1920), the first capitalists were pious Protestants who followed a strict moral code that was based on neighborly love. Because they honored hard work and believed in putting the profits from industrial activity toward the betterment of society, the Puritans strove to pursue their profits only through fair means. The ultimate purpose of their business activities was to contribute to society. The Puritan spirit of service to others and the world and their commitment to putting others before themselves thus formed the ethical foundation of early capitalism. In keeping with the Puritan business ethic, early capitalists exercised strict self-discipline and viewed helping others as their duty. As a result, the capitalist economy developed rapidly.

The Japanese philosopher Baigan Ishida (1685–1744) promoted a business principle that mirrors that of the Puritans. In the middle of the Edo period, Japan began to shift from a feudal peasant-based economy to a merchant-based commercial economy. Under the Japanese class system, however, merchants occupied the bottom rung of the social ladder and profit-driven commercial activity was frowned upon. In opposition of the prevailing view at the time, Baigan argued that there was no need to be ashamed of earning a profit. If it was legitimate for a samurai to receive a stipend, Baigan contended, it was just as legitimate for a merchant to receive profits from selling goods. His words greatly encouraged Japan's merchants, who were oppressed by social discrimination for their business activities.

Baigan also taught that the methods employed in the pursuit of profit must be based on the principle of fairness. He stressed the importance of following an ethical code in commercial activity, insisting that merchants should do what was right as a human being and refrain from stooping to unethical means to make money. "A true merchant," he stated, "thinks from the other's standpoint, not just his own." Baigan believed that the pursuit of profiting the customer as well as the merchant constituted the very core of business, which led to his claim that a spirit of "profiting self, profiting others" should drive all business activity.

Selflessness Widens Your Perspective

The pursuit of profit is the driving force behind business as well as many other human endeavors, and there is thus nothing wrong with wanting to make money. We should not pursue profit, however, for the benefit of ourselves alone. We need to "greedily" desire what is best for others and strive to promote the common good. If we do so, we too will benefit and the scope of our profit will greatly expand in the process.

Running a company, for example, is in itself a service to others and to society. Although the Japanese wage system, which is based on lifelong employment, is beginning to crumble, a company accepts its obligation to take responsibility for its hirees for most of their lives. Whether you have a staff of

5 people or 10, the act of employing those workers means that you are doing something for the benefit of others.

We also can be of service to others, and specifically to our families, in our personal lives. Before marriage, a man usually focuses solely on his own life, but when he marries and starts a family, his focus becomes working to support his wife and children. Through marriage, men's actions thus become oriented toward service to others even if the shift is only a subconscious one. We always must remain aware, however, that selfless service and personal gain occupy opposite sides of the same coin. If we look at our actions from a wider perspective, we will begin to see that a small act of service to others easily can become selfish.

When we do things for our family or our company, for example, we are engaging in selfless service to others, but as soon as we start focusing solely on profiting our own family or company without regard for others, our actions become egotistical and self-serving. If all we can think about is the good of our company, the effort we give to our work only serves to elevate the company's ego. The same is true for our family. It is therefore important to approach life from a broader perspective so that we can raise our acts of service to a higher level and see our actions in relation to the larger picture.

Instead of focusing on the good of our company, we should strive to run our business so that it also benefits our customers, consumers, shareholders, and the community. We should elevate our minds so that our sphere of selfless service broadens from individuals to our families, from our families to our communities, from our communities to society, from society to the country and the world, and from the world to the universe. If we broaden our perspective and become aware of what is happening around us, we will be able to make objective and sound decisions and avoid making mistakes.

Selflessness as a Motive for Starting a New Venture

The virtue of selflessness is a powerful driving force that can destroy obstacles and attract success to us. I experienced the power of virtue firsthand when I entered the telecommunications business in the early 1980s. Although competition among several companies is now the norm in the telecommunications field in Japan, in the 1980s the government-owned Nippon Telegraph and Telephone Corporation (NTT) monopolized the Japanese telecommunications market. As a result, user fees were much higher than those in other countries, and the Japanese government decided to deregulate the market to encourage competition.

Once NTT was privatized, other companies were free to enter the telecommunications market. No one, however, was willing to compete against NTT, and it continued to dominate the market. It was obvious that without healthy competition, user fees would not decrease and NTT would be privatized in name only. I felt compelled to do something. Although Kyocera was puny compared with NTT and had no experience in the telecommunications field, I realized if we sat idly by, the public would never enjoy the benefits that result from healthy marketplace competition. I knew competing with NTT would be like Don Quixote tilting at windmills, but I felt we should step forward and was confident that Kyocera, as a venture company, could take on the challenge.

I did not, however, express my intentions for my company right away. First, I needed to make absolutely sure that my motives for entering the telecommunications market were completely free from self-interest. I began asking myself every night before bed, "Are you really doing this for the public good? Are you sure that you aren't doing it for the company or for your own profit or because you want social recognition? Are your motives pure and completely unselfish?" I repeatedly examined my intentions.

Half a year later, finally certain that my intentions were free of self-interest, I plunged into establishing DDI (now KDDI). When Kyocera announced its decision to enter the telecommunications market, however, my employees and I found that two other companies also had decided to compete with NTT for market share. Of the three new contenders, DDI was considered the most likely to fail. This was understandable, for we were the only competing company with no telecommunications experience or technology. We would have to begin by establishing the technological infrastructure, such as cables and antennas, necessary for providers of telecommunications services, and we also would need to overcome the severe handicap of our lack of an established sales network.

Be Willing to Lose for the Sake of Others

Despite our disadvantages, DDI's sales consistently were the highest among the three contenders. I often am asked how DDI managed to succeed, but there is really only one answer: It was thanks to our selfless desire to be of service to the people of Japan.

From DDI's very beginning I continuously appealed to our employees, telling them that we had been given a once-in-a-lifetime opportunity. Through this project, I insisted, we could lower long-distance calling rates and in doing so be of great service to our fellow citizens. We should be grateful, I told them, for this opportunity and take full advantage of it. Everyone involved in DDI's formation shared this selfless resolve. They supported this project not for personal profit but for Japan, ardently longed for it to succeed, and dedicated themselves to achieving a favorable outcome. Our desire to be of service to others won us wide support from both sales agents and customers.

Not long after DDI was established, I offered employees the chance to buy shares in the venture at face value in order to reward their hard work and to express my appreciation. As the founder of the company, I could have become DDI's largest shareholder, but I chose not to own stock in the company because I believed that it would be wrong for me to have a selfish interest in DDI. If I had owned even a single share, I could not have defended myself against claims that I established DDI solely for the money. I also think that the company would have developed in a completely different direction.

The launch of DDI's cell phone business, which is known as au, was similar to the formation of DDI. From the time we established DDI, I was convinced that the cell phone market would have a future and eventually would make life much more convenient for everyone. But as soon as DDI branched into that market, we faced a major obstacle: Another company decided to enter the field at the same time as DDI. Ordinarily this would not have been a major issue. However, because Japan's broadcasting frequency restrictions allow the operation of only one other company besides NTT, DDI had to divide Japan's remaining coverage with the other company, forming two separate districts.

In terms of profitability, both companies naturally wanted market control over the densely populated cities and could not come to an agreement as to how to divide the districts. I suggested that drawing straws would be the fairest method of choosing coverage areas, but the Ministry of Posts and Telecommunications considered it unwise to leave such an important decision to chance. If the deadlock continued, the door to opportunity would never open. If someone did not give way, the mobile phone industry would never take root in Japan. I therefore suggested that DDI's competitor take coverage of the largest market, including major cities and the Chubu district, and we would take the nonurban areas.

DDI's board of directors demanded to know why I would give our rivals the meat and leave us with only the bun, but I reminded them of the saying "Lose a dime, win a dollar." I convinced the board that if we worked together, we could turn that dime into a pot of gold, and united we moved forward. Contrary to everyone's expectations, DDI's cell phone business grew rapidly, and au is now a close competitor with NTT DoCoMo.

I believe that the success of DDI and au is proof that the desire to be of service to others attracts the grace of God and always produces good results.

Business Profit Is a Trust; Use It for Society

Kyocera's management rationale is "to provide opportunities for the material and intellectual growth of all our employees and, through our joint efforts, contribute to the advancement of society and humankind." The goal of business management is first and foremost to provide a livelihood and ensure the well-being of the company's employees. However, if a company aspires to benefit only its employees, its pursuit of profit is destined to become selfish. A business is a public institution, and as such it has a responsibility to serve others and society. It was my sense of obligation to humankind that inspired me to add the second phrase to Kyocera's mission statement: It extends our management rationale from egocentric to altruistic.

I worked hard to create managerial altruism when I established Kyocera. Several years after the company's formation, as I handed my employees their year-end bonuses, I suggested that they contribute some of the money to society. I proposed that Kyocera would match the total amount of their donations and use the sum to buy food for people who could not afford to celebrate the new year. Our employees greeted my suggestion enthusiastically, marking the start of Kyocera's many subsequent charitable projects. Thus, from the very beginning, Kyocera has practiced and continues to maintain a spirit of service to others, contributing the fruits of our labor to the benefit of society.

On a personal level, in 1985 I contributed a total of 20 billion yen from my shares in Kyocera and other assets to establish the Inamori Foundation and the Kyoto Prize, an award that recognizes outstanding achievements in advanced technology, basic sciences, and arts and philosophy. I was motivated by my belief that the greatest human act is to contribute to society. The Kyoto Prize is widely recognized as an international honor, and in Japan it is equivalent to the Nobel Prize.

Although Kyocera's development brought me unexpected wealth, I knew my bounty was achieved only through the dedicated efforts and support of many people. Therefore, I did not consider these profits my private property. Rather, it seemed right to me to use the wealth given or, more accurately, entrusted to me to give back to society. The Kyoto Prize is thus my way of contributing to the world and at the same time an expression of my philosophy of service to others.

In 2003, the Carnegie Foundation presented me with the Andrew Carnegie Medal of Philanthropy in recognition of my charitable activities. Past recipients included notable philanthropists such as Bill Gates, George Soros, and Ted Turner, but I was the first Japanese person to receive the medal. During my acceptance speech, I explained that Kyocera and KDDI, the two enterprises I had built from the ground up, had achieved unimaginable growth, resulting in a large fortune. Because I shared Andrew Carnegie's belief that private wealth should be used for the public good, I explained in my speech, I felt compelled to use the wealth entrusted to me by Providence for the betterment of others and the world. The betterment of others is why I have promoted many social and philanthropic works during my lifetime.

Earlier I mentioned that the pursuit of profit must be fair, and I think that fairness should also be the basis for how we spread wealth. It is far more difficult to use wealth than it is to make it. Money made through a spirit of selfless service to others should be used in the same spirit, and it is only by spreading my wealth in the right way that I can effectively contribute to society.

Make Virtue-Based Wealth National Policy

Our attitude toward the events in our lives—whether we approach them with good intentions or bad—will determine the course our lives take. If, for example, you argue with someone about a problem with the intention of making the other person admit that the predicament is his fault, you will reach a very different conclusion than if you approached the other person with the desire to solve the problem and argued with him under the assumption that he must be struggling too. Your results are dependent upon whether you care about the person with whom you're arguing.

89

In the late 1990s, when trade restrictions were straining Japan's relations with the United States, I promoted the establishment of the U.S.-Japan 21st Century Committee, a bilateral forum in which people predominantly from the private sector could engage in frank discussions to improve the prospects for cooperation between the two nations. At the time, I proposed that participants from both sides of the divide refrain from antagonistic criticism and accusations.

I knew that the forum would accomplish nothing if people insisted on blaming one another or demanding that the other party make concessions. Discussions that are conducted with selfish motives, the desire to win, or disregard of the other person's position or background are fruitless and only deepen mutual distrust. I therefore suggested that the forum members respect each person's position and listen with consideration to everyone's point of view without clinging to their own opinions, that we conduct our discussions with an attitude of selfless consideration for others.

I also suggested that if necessary, Japan should take the lead in making concessions because the United States had been very generous to Japan in the aftermath of World War II. The Americans ungrudgingly provided Japan with food and technology and opened their extensive market to Japanese products, allowing Japan to rebuild and grow. Even if their postwar actions were part of the United States' global strategy, the fact remained that they had treated us with extreme generosity, so it was Japan's turn to reciprocate. It was, I felt, Japan's duty as a major economic nation to acquire the spirit of selflessness and generosity that is needed to reach a compromise.

The U.S.-Japan 21st Century Committee carried out discussions over a two-year period and submitted a final report on its conclusions to the governments of both countries. The forum's results indicate that the keys to the future design of Japan are the spirit of consideration for others and the cultivation of virtue. Heita Kawakatsu (1948–), a professor at the International Research Center for Japanese Studies, has proposed that a prosperous nation such as Japan should be founded on virtue, not wealth, and that a country's wealth should be utilized in an ethical way to contribute to other people and nations. By using good deeds instead of military might or economic power, we gain the trust and respect of other nations.

I agree. Virtue should be the basis of national policy. Japan has experienced the aftermath that results from selfishly pursuing domestic profit alone. We therefore should take the lead and think of the welfare of other nations first, providing an example to others. Rather than trying to become an economic or military superpower, we should aspire to virtue-based nation building.

Instead of excelling in mathematical calculations or busying ourselves with flaunting our military strength, we should build a firm foundation of national ethics that reflects the noble spirit of human virtues. It is from this standpoint that we should interact with the world.

If we base our national policy on virtue above all else, Japan truly will be needed and respected in international society. It is also very unlikely that any country will want to invade us, which makes virtue the ultimate security policy.

Have We Forgotten Essential Virtues?

Sun Yat-sen (1866–1925), a Chinese revolutionary who often is referred to as the father of modern China, gave a famous speech in Kobe in 1924 regarding Pan-Asianism. The culture of ruling by military force—the rule of might, as the ancients called it—he maintained, originated in the West. In contrast, Asian civilization was based on the rule of right or the kingly way, in which leaders guided their people with virtue. Yat-sen urged Japan, which was heading down the path of the rule of might, to choose the kingly way.

Unfortunately, Japan failed to change its course and rushed headlong into World War II. Since its defeat, the country has continued on a path ruled by might, but this time its pursuit is economic supremacy. Now, however, it is time for Japan and the Japanese people to choose the kingly way and adopt the virtues of consideration and service to others as their standard for living. If we don't, I fear that Japan will continue to make grave mistakes.

There is a saying in the Tendai sect of Buddhism, "*Mohko rita*," which can be translated as "forget self, serve others." The Tendai priest Etai Yamada (1900–1999) taught me that this saying urges us to set our own selves aside and devote ourselves to serving others. I feel strongly that Japanese society is in danger of losing the important cultural virtues of consideration and selfless service. If we forget these virtues, all we have left are selfish desires, the negative results of which we already are witnessing in Japan.

A few years ago, a 19-year-old youth was convicted of killing a family of four and was sentenced to death for his crime despite the fact that he was still considered a minor under Japanese law and thus should not have been subject to the death penalty. It became apparent during the youth's trial that his crime was pre-meditated and was carried out based on his assumption that his status as a minor would afford him a lighter sentence. A reporter commented that if he had known the law, the youth might not have committed murder. Before knowing the law, however, what this boy needed to know was the fundamental moral and ethical principle that we should not kill. The prohibition against killing is not merely a law; it is a moral standard for living as human beings.

Education Must Shift to Morality-Based Character Training

How did we lose our basic moral standards? How could we forget the spirit of consideration and selfless service? The answer is simple: Adults failed to teach these principles to their children. The majority of Japanese people born in the 60 years that have passed since the end of World War II were never taught moral values. I know this because I was born and given a moral education before the war.

In postwar Japan, personal autonomy has been overempha-sized and subjected to too much individualized interpretation. Children have been given too much freedom without learning that with freedom comes responsibility. Postwar Japanese society has neglected to acquire the virtues that make us human and resultantly failed to internalize the basic rules required to live in society.

In the past, religion provided human beings with the philosophy that served as a compass for life. The teachings of Buddhism, Christianity, and other religions gave us a moral standard for living. They taught us that God or the Buddha is watching over us, ensuring that if we do something bad, we will get what we deserve. Similarly, these teachings informed us that God or the Buddha never abandons those who do good deeds regardless of whether those deeds are noticed by others. These religious tenets forced us to think about the ethics of our actions. With the development of scientific civilization, however, religion has been ignored and we gradually have forgotten the moral, ethical, and philosophical principles that once guided us.

The philosopher Takeshi Umehara (1925–) claimed that the moral decline of society has been caused by a lack of religion, and I agree. In postwar Japan there was a strong push to eliminate morals and ethics from daily life and education in retroaction to the thought control exerted by State Shinto during World War II. Even now, although there has been much fanfare about instituting a comprehensive educational system in Japan, very little attempt is being made to build our children's characters through moral education at school. In addition, Japan's postwar overemphasis on fostering individuality has resulted in children not receiving proper instruction in the most basic rules and morals. Even kindergartens are advocating liberal education, and children who are too young to understand moral concepts are left to their own devices, denied the opportunity to learn the most basic and necessary social rules before they grow up.

Children and teenagers must be given the opportunity to think about what it means to be human and to live rightly when they are developing physically, intellectually, and emotionally. In addition, education must foster a proper understanding of the meaning of work. In Japanese society, a person's educational background determines his or her worth. Children who excel at their studies are separated from those who don't and are given preferential treatment. As a result, young people have a warped view of work. Good grades and a job with the government or a major business firm are idealized whereas nonacademic skills such as dexterity and the ability to get along with others are neglected.

To counteract this trend, we need to teach our children that there is a tremendous diversity of occupations and that it is the dedicated efforts of each individual in her particular job that make daily life and progress possible. On this basis, we can give a child who aspires to be a hairdresser the practical knowledge he needs to serve that occupation. This is the kind of vocational education we need to provide for our youth.

It does not matter what one's occupation is. Hard work in one's profession, regardless if it is shrine carpentry, cabinetmaking, tailoring, farming, fishing, and so on, is the means for refining our souls and elevating our characters. Fostering an understanding of what it means to work should be a major focus of the educational system.

Learn from Past Mistakes; Build a New Japan

Since entering the modern era, Japan seems to have faced a major turning point in its history once every 40 years. In 1868, with the start of the Meiji Restoration, Japan emerged from feudalism and began building a modern nation, racing toward a vision of prosperity and military might. In 1905, Japan won a war against Russia, becoming a global power and dramatically increasing its international status. The victory accelerated Japan's push to build its military strength and launched the nation on the path of militarism and conquest. In 1945, Japan lost World War II. From the ashes of defeat, Japan changed direction yet again and began to focus on the pursuit of wealth, which resulted in phenomenal economic growth for the country. In 1985, Japan signed the Plaza Accord to devalue the American dollar in relation to the yen and alleviate the trade deficit, marking the peak of Japan's economic power. The Plaza Accord was followed by the collapse of the bubble economy and a long-term recession.

Looking back on these 40-year cycles of prosperity and decline, it is clear that Japan repeatedly has entered into competition with other nations in the pursuit of material wealth. In particular, after World War II, when economic growth was the country's supreme goal, Japanese companies and individuals enthusiastically sought ways to increase their profits, a focus that has continued to this day. The prolonged stagnation of the Japanese society and economy requires Japan to drastically change the direction of the country, yet the Japanese people still are racing to get ahead. Their only standard is the increase of profit, so they swing from hope to despair at the slightest fluctuation in the gross domestic product (GDP).

Japan is pursuing profit without any moral guidelines and living by the rule of might, wherein motivation is driven by greed and priority is given to material affluence through survival of the fittest. We have yet to extricate ourselves from this way of governing and living.

It has become clear, however, that Japan's current value system has reached a dead end. If we continue to base our national identity on unbridled economic growth, we will be stuck forever in the same vicious cycle, spinning in a downward spiral at an unstoppable speed until our moral standards sink even lower than they did at the end of World War II. Our expanding local and national deficits, the snail's pace of administrative reform, and the decline in social vitality that is accompanying the falling birthrate all are signs of Japan's ominous future. By the time Japan reaches the beginning of its next 40-year cycle in 2025, it could be faced with a crisis that will destroy the nation rather than presented with a hopeful vision of the future. This is the time to establish new national ideals and a new guideline for personal living that will replace Japan's current emphasis on economic growth.

Our collective lust for greed and growth affects more than just Japan's economy. In fact, the urgent and enormous issues that confront international society—and even the environment— find their roots in our rampant pursuit of profit. If we refuse to relinquish our unbridled greed for limitless growth and consumption, we will not only exhaust the limited resources of the planet but also destroy the environment on which we depend. If we continue on our current course, we will not only bankrupt our nation but also destroy with our own hands our common home: the earth. We must realize that it is futile to seek luxury and material pleasures while our boat is sinking and urgently rechart our course on the basis of a new philosophy.

Learning Contentment from the Laws of Nature

But what is this new philosophy? Within what philosophical soil should Japan and its people set down their roots? Personally, I believe we should base our way of life on contentment and, with the gratitude and humility this will generate, seek to care for and serve others.

The world of nature is an excellent model of contentment. Plants are eaten by herbivores, which in turn are eaten by carnivores. The dung and carcasses of these carnivorous animals return to the earth and nourish the plants. Looked at from a larger perspective, even the principle of survival of the fittest is encompassed within the harmony of nature's cycle.

Unlike human beings, animals do not attempt to break the chain of life. If the amount herbivores ate was dictated by greed, they would devour every last plant and destroy the cycle of nature, threatening the lives of all living things. Instead, they are equipped with an instinctive control that prevents them from overeating. Similarly, in response to the Creator's will, lions instinctually do not hunt when they are full. It is because living creatures in nature adhere to the principle of contentment that the harmony and stability of the natural world have been maintained for so long.

We should learn moderation from nature. As former residents of the natural world, we once lived within the chain of life and must have understood its guiding principle of moderation very well. However, when we freed ourselves from the yoke of the food chain and stepped beyond the restrictions of the laws that govern the environment, we lost the humility to seek coexistence with other forms of life.

97

Out of all creation, human beings alone have been endowed with "higher" intelligence. Our mental sophistication has allowed us not only to mass-produce food and industrial products but to develop technology that makes our production processes more efficient. At some point in time, however, our intelligence turned into arrogance and swelled our selfish desire to control nature. Moderation, which once helped us feel content, vanished, and our greed for wealth has run unchecked and brought the earth to the brink of destruction.

When Humankind Awakens, a Civilization of Selflessness Will Flourish

To keep this ship called Planet Earth from sinking, we have no choice but to regain our natural sense of moderation. We must transform the intelligence God has bestowed upon us into true wisdom and learn to control our desires. We need to practice the spirit of contentment in our daily lives, knowing that if we can't be content with what we have been given, we will never find satisfaction, even if we manage to fulfill our every desire.

It is time to stop pursuing profit and free the goals of the nation and the individual from the confinement of material wealth. Instead, we should explore how we can all live together harmoniously while enriching our souls. This is the way of contentment. In the words of the ancient Chinese philosopher Laozi, "He who knows contentment has wealth." Contentment is the true philosopher's stone. If you can't obtain what you want, want what you can obtain.

We need to practice the spirit of contentment because it is the key to world stability. It also keeps our selfish desires in check and allows us to be content with less so that we can share what we have with others. Contentment means maintaining a loving and generous spirit that rejoices in the fulfillment of others. You may call me naive and idealistic, but I truly believe that the attitude of contentment will save Japan and the world.

Contentment, however, does not mean being complacent or accepting current conditions without attempting anything new. It does not equate with stagnation or defeatism. Rather, contentment can be compared to the GDP. Although the total sum may remain the same, its content, or its industrial structure, is changing constantly. Old industries may die out, but new ones will arise to take their place. It is a dynamic, vital, and creative way of life in which human wisdom constantly is generating new ideas and rejuvenating itself.

It is in this state of contentment that we can shift from growth to maturity, from competition to coexistence, and walk the path of harmony. As we traverse this path, we will witness the birth of a new civilization that is motivated by the virtue of selfless service to others. The driving force behind our current civilization is the desire for more: more leisure, more food, more money. In contrast, the new civilization will be based on love and consideration for others, the desire to help others grow and make them happy.

I don't know exactly what form this civilization will take or what its contents will be. Perhaps it is just a pipe dream. But I am convinced that it is not the creation of this new civilization that is important but rather the daily effort we make to build it. It is the process of getting there, not being there, that refines our souls. If we elevate our minds by striving to create a new, more loving civilization, I believe that the path to a service-oriented society will be far shorter than we ever imagined.

CHAPTER 5

TUNING IN TO THE
FLOW OF THE UNIVERSE

Two Invisible Forces That Govern Our Lives

I believe that there are two invisible forces that govern our lives. One of those forces is destiny. Each person is born into this world with his or her own destiny, and although we do not know what our specific fate is, it leads and at times pushes us through life. Some people will disagree, but I believe its existence is undeniable. Destiny, which is beyond the reach of our will and desires, governs our lives and propels us along without regard for our feelings, like a great river flowing ceaselessly to the boundless ocean.

But does destiny render us powerless over our lives? I don't believe so, because there is another invisible hand that guides our life's journey: the universal law of cause and effect, an extremely simple law that directly joins causes to results. Good deeds produce good results, and bad deeds produce bad results.

All the circumstances in our lives are born of causes, and all our thoughts and deeds are the causes that bear the fruit of our circumstances. If you are thinking about something or doing something right now, whatever it is, it will serve as a cause that will produce some kind of result. Moreover, your responses to the results that your thoughts and deeds beget will create still more consequences in your life. Our lives cycle through and are governed by this endless series of chain reactions, by the universal law of cause and effect.

The law of cause and effect can be tied back to our discussion from Chapter 1, wherein we asserted that we attract only those things on which we focus and that life is an expression of our minds. Like seeds, our thoughts and actions generate a specific reality. Cause and effect also relates back to Chapter 3, which included a discussion on the importance of refining and elevating the mind. If we follow the law of cause and effect and purify and elevate our minds, we resultantly will have better lives.

Destiny and the law of cause and effect—these are the two great principles that govern our lives. Destiny is the warp and cause and effect is the woof in the cloth of life we weave. Our lives do not turn out exactly as they were destined to thanks to cause and effect, and conversely, good deeds do not always lead immediately to good results when destiny intervenes. It is important to remember, however, that the law of cause and effect has a little more power over the course of our lives than does destiny. Thus, we can reroute the flow of our destiny in a positive direction if we put the principle of cause and effect to good use and think good thoughts and do good deeds. Although we are controlled to some extent by our destiny, our thoughts and deeds have the power to change our life's course.

Understand the Law of Cause and Effect and Change Your Destiny

I first encountered the idea of consciously using the law of cause and effect in *Fate and Establishing One's Destiny* by Masahiro

Yasuoka (1898–1983), a Confucian scholar who influenced many Japanese politicians and economists. In his book, Yasuoka relates the classic Chinese tale of Liao-Fan. The story, which was written more than four centuries ago, goes like this:

Liao-Fan was born to a family of doctors. His father died when he was young, and his mother raised him single-handedly. During his youth, Liao-Fan began studying medicine, in the tradition of his forefathers. One day an elderly man came to visit. "I have mastered the art of fortune-telling," the elderly man said, "and in obedience to the command of heaven, I have come to tell you the essence of what I have learned." The elderly man then turned to Liao-Fan's mother and said: "I expect that you're planning to train this boy in medicine, but he isn't destined to become a doctor. When he grows up, Liao-Fan will take the imperial exams and become a government official." The elderly man further predicted not only the age at which Liao-Fan would take the exams and the grades he would score but also that he would be appointed regional governor while still young, rise to a very high rank, marry but never have children, and finally die at the age of 53.

Liao-Fan's life unfolded exactly as the elderly man had foretold. One day when Liao-Fan had become the regional governor, he visited a renowned Zen master and asked to join him in meditation. The Zen master was amazed at Liao-Fan's ability to slip into deep meditation without becoming distracted. "You have reached such a high level of consciousness. Where on earth did you train?" he asked.

Liao-Fan answered that he had received no training and then told him about the elderly man he had met in his youth. "My life has unfolded exactly as that man foretold. It is my destiny to die at 53, and therefore there is no point in worrying about the future."

The Zen master rebuked Liao-Fan sternly: "I was impressed that you had reached enlightenment at such a young age, but now I know that you are just a fool! Do you intend to live your life as destiny dictates? True, destiny is God-given, but that does not mean we can't change it. If you think good thoughts and do good deeds, you can transcend your destiny and turn your life in an even better direction."

Liao-Fan took this explanation of the universal law of cause and effect to heart and thereafter strove to do good deeds, not bad. As it turned out, he was blessed with a child and lived well beyond the age that had been predicted.

We too can change our destiny with our own actions. If we strive to think positive thoughts and do good deeds, we can activate the law of cause and effect and create an even better life than the one that has been destined for us. As noted in Chapter 1, we should strive to practice what Masahiro Yasuoka referred to as *ritsumei*, or aligning the course of our lives with the ultimate reality. Not many people, however, believe in *ritsumei*, and the vast majority scoff at the concept, considering it unscientific. It isn't possible to use modern scientific criteria to prove the existence of life's two invisible governing forces. When looked at in the light of modern reason, the idea of destiny appears to be mere superstition and the law of cause and effect sounds like a tale concocted to frighten children and warn them that if they don't behave, God will punish them.

If good deeds instantly and always produced good results, people would perhaps believe in both destiny and cause and effect, but this almost never happens. It is very rare that a positive action today will produce a correspondingly positive result tomorrow. Unlike a mathematical equation in which one plus one always equals two, the relationship between cause A and effect B is rarely obvious because destiny and cause and effect operate jointly to weave the tapestry of our lives. They mutually interact with each other. If destiny happens to be leading us through a very bad period in our lives, the effect of a positive act may be too small to counteract destiny's negative influence or produce visible results. Conversely, if destiny is leading us through a very positive period in our lives, the impact of insignificant negative actions may be only very slight.

Cause and Effect Always Balance Out

Because they can't see the instantaneous results of their positive actions, people find it difficult to believe in the law of cause and effect. However, rewards from good deeds do not come in a very short time span. It takes time for the effects of our thoughts and actions to bear fruit. In most cases, two or three years is too short a period. If we look at our lives in intervals of 20 to 30 years, however, it becomes clear that cause and effect always balance out.

105

More than 40 years have passed since I established Kyocera, during which time I have seen many people go through various ups and downs in their lives. Over that span of three or four decades, however, the end results of each person's life almost always matched his or her daily actions and way of living. In the long run, misfortune does not last for people who are sincere and willing to help others and prosperity does not stay with those who are lazy and indifferent. On the surface, some people seem to lead successful lives despite living badly whereas others who always do the right thing constantly seem to experience temporary misfortune; however, as time passes, people's life circumstances are gradually corrected until their results eventually match the way they have lived their lives and their situations eventually match who they are as human beings. At that point, it is almost as if there were an equal sign between cause and effect. In the long run, good deeds always bear good fruit and, conversely, bad deeds always bear bad fruit.

Several years ago, Kyocera helped reconstruct Mita Industries, a struggling copier manufacturer. Under Kyocera's guidance, Mita Industries' business performance improved dramatically, and the company paid off its huge debts much sooner than expected. The company improved so much that Kyocera and Mita Industries eventually decided to come together and establish a new company, named Kyocera Mita Corporation, and that company is now a pillar of the Kyocera Group.

Reconstructing a company, however, is not always an easy task. Twenty years ago, Kyocera had to reconstruct an up-and-coming information equipment manufacturer. The company had seen rapid initial growth in response to a boom in demand, but soon thereafter, as its demand declined and business dropped, the firm was forced to reach out to Kyocera for help. The Kyocera Group eventually took responsibility for the manufacturer and its employees, including several radical extremist labor union members. Even though Kyocera had rescued their company and its employees from disaster, the extremists made unreasonable demands, accosted me at my home, and spread malicious slander, making my life extremely unpleasant and severely damaging Kyocera's reputation. All I could do was to endure the situation as best as I could. As time passed, however, many of the employees from the reconstructed company came to understand Kyocera's position and expressed their gratitude to Kyocera and me for saving their jobs. It was one of those people—the former plant manager at the information equipment manufacturer—who, 20 years later, became the first president of Kyocera Mita and directed its reconstruction, greatly contributing to its success. Once in the position of being rescued, the new president of Kyocera Mita was now in the position of saving others. Deeply moved by this turn of events, he told me, "I was once saved, and now I am saving others. I can't help but feel the hand of destiny in this. By helping rebuild Mita Industries, I have been given a chance to return the kindness that was once shown to me. I'm overjoyed."

The words of this man confirmed for me yet again the fact that over the long term good deeds bring good results. When Kyocera was in the midst of reconstructing the information equipment manufacturer, our difficulties seemed horrendous, but we succeeded in rebuilding the business and were rewarded by the appreciation of the employees. My experience of reconstructing the manufacturing company convinced me that this circle of goodness would expand in the future, and 20 years later, I was proven right.

Caigentan (*Vegetable Root Discourse*), a Chinese classic from the Ming dynasty, compares good deeds that seem to go unrewarded to gourds growing in long grass. They may be invisible to our eyes, but nevertheless they are growing very well. We should remember that it takes time for the effects of our positive actions to become visible and strive untiringly and steadily to do good without growing impatient to see the results.

The Universe Constantly Promotes the Growth of All Things

The law of cause and effect is a governing force in our lives because it is in accordance with the laws of nature. As the process by which the universe was created clearly demonstrates, it is the will of the universe that good deeds always produce good fruits and never bad ones whereas bad deeds always produce bad results and never good ones. My logic is as follows:

In the field of astrophysics, the dominant theory concerning the origin of the universe is the Big Bang. According to the

Big Bang theory, an infinitely hot, dense clump of elementary particles inflated and expanded about 13 billion years ago to form a continually expanding universe. The universe, like a single organism, continues to grow (expand) today.

During the Big Bang, the matter of the universe was created through a series of seemingly impossible events. First, elementary particles, including protons, mesons, and neutrons, formed and were joined together to create atomic nuclei, which then combined with electrons to give rise to the first atoms. Individual atoms next began linking up with other individual atoms through nuclear fusion to form altogether new types of atoms, and when certain types of atoms combined with other types of atoms, molecules came into existence. Molecules then fused into macromolecules, and when DNA was introduced into those macromolecules, life was born. Over a mind-boggling span of time, primordial forms of life evolved into higher organisms, which eventually developed into the human race. The history of the universe is thus a dynamic process of evolutionary development from elementary particles to higher organisms.

But why did evolution occur? The original elementary particles just as easily could have stayed the way they were or could have stopped evolving after becoming atoms. Why did evolution continue without pause, generating one life-form after another until the human race emerged? Some claim that the induction of life into the universe was accidental, but it would have been extremely unnatural for unceasing growth and evolution to occur simply by chance and without any purpose. It is more logical to postulate that evolution was inevitable, the result of divine will. At least that's what I think.

There is a well-intentioned will or force in the universe that acts like a current of energy, continuously propelling the growth and development of all things, guiding all matter, both organic and inorganic, including the human race, in a positive direction. It is the will of the universe that promotes the law of cause and effect, in which good deeds produce positive results, and it was the will of the universe that initiated the evolutionary process, which began with the fusion of elementary particles into atoms, molecules, and macromolecules and continues to this day. It is the will of the universe that guides all things in a positive direction and encourages their growth and development—the universe overflows with love and mercy.

Aligning our attitudes and our ways of life with the great will of the universe (love), therefore, is of the utmost importance. Good thoughts and good deeds fulfill the intentions of the universe, and so it is only natural that they should bring wonderful results into our lives. Everything I have discussed in this book so far—gratitude and sincerity, diligence and open-mindedness, self-reflection, the avoidance of envy, the spirit of selfless service to others—all these good thoughts and deeds are in accordance with the will of the universe and inevitably will guide us to success, development, and a great destiny. The success or failure of our lives and of all our endeavors is determined by whether we are aligned to this will, to the flow of the universe.

It's a simple principle: The universe desires the betterment of all things and hence accelerates the growth and development of everything that exists within it. Human beings are no exception; therefore, if our attitudes and ways of life match the will of the universe, we are guaranteed the best results in our lives and work.

A Great Force Breathes Life into All Things

The existence of life is not the result of a combination of coincidences but rather is the inevitable product of the will of the universe. This idea is not that unusual. Kazuo Murakami

109

(1936–), professor emeritus at the University of Tsukuba and one of the world's top geneticists, was forced to conclude from his genetic research that a mysterious will beyond our comprehension governs the universe.

Amazingly, the genetic codes of all living things, from simple bacteria all the way to complex organisms such as human beings, are encoded in differing sequences of only four chemical letters. Moreover, the information contained in a single gene is equivalent to a combination of 3 billion of those letters. If we were to print any given organism's genetic code for only one gene in book form, the end result would be a 3,000-volume-long tome, with each volume containing 1,000 pages. When you consider the fact that genetic information is written within every single one of the approximately 60 trillion cells that make up the average human being, you can begin to understand the complexity of life.

The microscopic size of the DNA that contains our genetic information is equally amazing. If you collected the DNA from all 6 billion people living on this earth, the aggregate weight would be equivalent to that of only a single grain of rice—that is how little space this vast amount of information occupies.

These facts are nothing short of miraculous. It is virtually impossible for a phenomenon with this degree of complexity to occur by coincidence. The only conceivable explanation for the existence of life is the reality and operation of a force that far transcends human understanding, a force that Murakami calls "Something Great." Human beings can't understand this "Something Great," but it created the universe and life. Some call it God. I call it the will of the universe. But whatever we call it—and even if we can't understand it—we should acknowledge its existence. Otherwise, the evolution of the universe and the mysterious and exquisite mechanism of life cannot be explained.

We borrow our life force from this great being, from the will of the universe. The life-giving energy that emanates from the hand of the Creator is omnipresent in the universe and constantly breathes life into all things. It is the manifestation of the universe's love and power, which desires to give all things life.

I remember feeling the will of the universe 30 years ago when Kyocera succeeded in synthesizing recrystallized gems, which are made from the same natural elements as natural gems. To make an emerald, for example, we melt metal oxides at high temperatures and then slowly cool them. As the red-hot material cools, we add a small natural crystal into the molten metal oxide as a seed from which the recrystallized emerald grows. However, it is very difficult to determine the exact moment at which the crystal should be added. If we add the natural crystal too soon, it melts, and if we add it too late, the crystal won't grow. It took seven years of trial and error before we succeeded in creating recrystallized gems. When we timed the process exactly right, we could see the small crystal grow as if it were really alive. It was as if an invisible hand were guiding this process.

As Kyocera's experience with growing crystals shows, there is something in the universe that makes inanimate matter seem alive, a quiet but powerful will, a desire, love, force, or energy that wants all things to live. We cannot see this force, but we can feel it. It is omnipresent in limitless space; it is the source of all life and presides over birth, growth, and extinction. It is the mother, the driving force of all circumstances and experience. It matters not what you call this unfathomable power: the will of the universe, "Something Great," the invisible hand of the Creator. It cannot be measured by scientific criteria, but trust me when I say that you must believe that this force exists and live your life accordingly. Ultimately, choosing to believe in this great power will determine the success or failure of your life; it

111

can free you from the evils of arrogance and foster humility and goodness inside of you.

Choosing to Become a Buddhist Priest

Why were we created and sent into this world by the Creator? Why were we given the opportunity to live just once and endowed with the innate capacity to continuously grow and develop? To rephrase this question, how should we live our lives so that we are in accordance with the will of the universe?

This is a profound question that exceeds human understanding, yet I believe that nature created us for no other purpose than as follows: We should elevate our minds and increase the nobility of our souls so that both are a little better, a little more beautiful when we die than they were when we were born, and we should strive until our last breath to have good thoughts, do good deeds, and build our characters.

Any wealth, fame, or rank that we acquire in this world is meaningless if we do not live according to the will of the universe. It doesn't matter how successful we are in life, how brilliant our business achievements are, or how great the fortune we amass is. Compared with the importance of elevating our minds, these accomplishments are as worthless as trash. The final goal of human life as decreed by the will of the universe is to refine our souls. This life is given to us solely as a training ground for that purpose.

As I have explained in this book, if we are to refine and elevate our minds, we must constantly strive in our daily lives to practice the *Rokuharamitsu* (Six Perfections) taught by the Buddha, including *fuse*, *jikai*, *shojin*, *ninniku*, *zenjo*, and *chie*. I have always felt the inherent truth of the Six Perfections throughout the course of my life, but when I turned 65, I decided to enter the Buddhist priesthood and learn more about the meaning of life. I wanted to gain real faith. I had planned to join the Buddhist priesthood at age 60, but my sixtieth birthday coincided with the launching of Kyocera's cell phone venture and other important projects, and so I was not free to do as I wished. When I was nearing 65, however, I decided that I couldn't put off the priesthood any longer, retired from the front line and assume only chairman emeritus of both Kyocera and DDI, and became a lay priest.

I have always thought of my life as being divided into three parts. Assuming that I would live 80 years, I estimated that the first 20 years of my life would be spent learning to take care of myself. The next 40 years, from age 20 to age 60, would be devoted to working for others and society while refining my character. The final 20 years, from age 60 to age 80, would be spent preparing to die; that is, preparing for the journey of the soul. Just as it took 20 years to prepare to go out into the world to work, I figured that it would take 20 years to prepare to leave it.

Although death involves the destruction of the physical body, the soul is eternal. Because I believe this, I see death as the soul embarking on a new journey. I wanted to prepare for it properly, and so I entered the priesthood to further my study of the meaning of life.

Imperfection Is Normal; It Is the Effort That Counts

Entering the priesthood and training to become a priest were deeply moving and sacred experiences. Through practices such as *takuhatsu* (begging for alms) I was touched by the mercy of the Buddha. In some ways, my time in the priesthood taught me to view the world with new eyes, whereas in other ways I recognized that I could continue living my life just as I always had. There is a Zen saying: "Before enlightenment, I cut wood and carried water. After enlightenment, I cut wood and carried water." Even after entering the priesthood, I continue to be immersed in the dust and dross of the secular world, but I feel with certainty that my time as a lay Buddhist priest has changed me inside.

Through ascetic practice, for example, I became keenly aware of the immaturity I held in my heart. As the head of Kyocera, I managed executives and subordinates and issued them instructions. I wrote books and gave speeches, behaving as if I were an expert in my field. But Buddhist practice made me realize that I could be irresponsible and disagreeable at times, an awareness that caused me to pause and reflect. I further was struck by my realization that those that should be respected as truly outstanding people—those with pure hearts—almost always go unknown and unrecognized. A true hero, I learned, might be a kind elderly person living in a back alley or a youth who is striving toward a goal in the big city. I came to see that such people are vastly superior to, and their love for others is far greater than that of, people who have acquired fame, fortune, and success.

Paradoxically, I also learned that ordinary people like me will never reach enlightenment. No matter how hard we try, it is simply impossible. During the priesthood initiation ceremony, a Buddhist priest asks each initiate if he or she will obey 10 precepts. The moment I affirmatively responded that I would obey the precepts, I became a priest. Yet, even though I vowed to obey the precepts, which consequently granted me acceptance into the Buddhist priesthood, I don't think it's possible to follow the priesthood's rules completely. No matter how diligently I try, even if I sit meditating for hundreds of hours, I cannot attain enlightenment. Someone who is as weak-willed as I am, who has as much difficulty separating himself from worldly desires as I do, will never be able to put others first at all times. No matter how hard we try to follow the precepts of the Buddhist priesthood, we are bound to break them because as human beings we are foolish and imperfect.

What I came to understand is that human imperfection is okay. We still can strive for perfection even if in the end we will never be able to succeed. The effort itself is noble. Even if we are never able to obey life's precepts perfectly, our desire to obey, our feeling that we must obey, and our exercise of sincere self-reflection and discipline when we fail to obey are what is truly important. Through religious practice, I came to believe that even if we don't reach enlightenment, if we live each day working to become better people, we will be better able to refine our souls and achieve salvation.

It is not people who have achieved great things but people who are trying to achieve great things that God, the Buddha, and the will of the universe love. They will help those who try but fail, who reflect on their shortcomings and resolve to try again tomorrow. Can we refine our souls just by trying? The answer is yes. Will we still be saved? Again, the answer is yes. The noble process of desiring and constantly striving to elevate our souls hones our characters. Why? Simply because continually working to better ourselves is in accordance with the mercy of the Buddha and the will of the universe.

The Beauty of the True Self

I think of the mind as consisting of multilayered concentric circles that are arranged in order from the outside in, as follows:

1. *Intellect*: the knowledge and logic acquired after birth
2. *Sensation*: the part of the mind that governs the psychological effects of the five senses, our emotions, and so on
3. *Instinct*: the desires and urges that maintain our physical bodies

4. *Soul*: the true self clad in temporal experiences and karma
5. *True self*: the core, which is located at the very center and is filled with truth, goodness, and beauty

The core of our consciousness is the true self, and it is surrounded in the mind by the soul. At birth, the true self and the soul become wrapped in the layer of instinct. A newborn baby that seeks its mother's milk, for example, does so instinctually, using the outermost part of its mind. As the baby grows, its mind develops a layer of sensation around instinct, which is then followed by the formation of the mind's intellect. In other words, as a person matures, additional aspects of the mind are added layer by layer to the true self at the center.

When we grow old, the layers of our minds are stripped away from the outside in. As senility sets in, the powers of the intellect and reasoning decline until, like a child, our emotions become the guiding layer of our minds. Subsequently, our emotions and sensation are dulled and our instinct surfaces and fades as we come closer and closer to death.

The most important layers of our minds are those that form its center: the true self and the soul. The true self is the core of our existence, our true consciousness. In Buddhism, the true self is called *chie*, or the eternal truth of the universe, and when we reach *chie*, when we achieve enlightenment, we can understand all the truths that penetrate the universe. *Chie*, in other words, is a projection of the desire of the Buddha, of God; it is the manifestation of the will of the universe.

Buddhism teaches that the nature of the Buddha resides in all things. A person's true self is the nature of the Buddha, the wisdom of the universe, the essence of all that is, the truth of creation. And because it is the nature of the Buddha, the true self is incomparably beautiful. It overflows with the virtues of love, sincerity, harmony, truth, goodness, and beauty. Because they form the core of the mind, of the true self, these virtues are naturally desirable to human beings, and therefore we can't help longing for them.

When Adversity Strikes, Rejoice, for Your Karma Is Gone

The true self is wrapped in the soul. If we think of the true self as the pure "naked" self, it wears as its garment the soul, which is woven from our desires and deeds, from everything in our consciousness and everything we experience, from all the things we have ever cared about and accomplished in the world. In other words, the soul includes all the good thoughts and bad thoughts, all the good deeds and bad deeds we have accumulated throughout our many lives: our karma. Although the true self is common to all, the constitution of each person's soul is different.

In Kagoshima, where I grew up, the expression "You have a bad soul" often was used to refer to someone that was always complaining or weak-willed, and I remember my mother repeating this expression to me when I was a small child. I'm guessing that my mother told me I had a bad soul because she saw that it was a little crooked or impure as a result of bad karma.

But what is karma, which clings like dust to the soul? Tansetsu Nishikata, the elderly priest who guided my initiation into the Buddhist priesthood, taught me a profound lesson about karma more than 20 years ago. At that time, Kyocera was the target of heavy criticism for manufacturing and selling a fine ceramic artificial knee joint before securing regulatory approval. The backlash against Kyocera seemed rather unfair. After all, Kyocera had developed the ceramic artificial knee joint using

117

applied technology from an artificial hip joint that had already received regulatory approval. What's more, we had created the new medical product at the ardent request of many doctors. Still, I did not try to defend myself but instead resolved to accept my misfortune.

When I visited Tansetsu, I remarked, "This problem is causing me so much stress."

Tansetsu had read about Kyocera's problem in the newspaper, and I was expecting him to say something sympathetic. Instead he said, "It must be hard, but it can't be helped. Living always entails some suffering. When you meet adversity, don't be sad. You should rejoice. Through suffering, the karma that clings to your soul is erased. Mr. Inamori, you should be celebrating. The kind of difficulty you're facing right now is enough to wipe away your karma."

Tansetsu's words were such a relief to me. He gave me exactly what I needed: a lesson that was far more calming than any words of sympathy could ever be. Tansetsu's sage advice taught me about the meaning of life and showed me a great deep-rooted truth about the nature of karma.

Instead of Seeking Enlightenment, Use Reason and Conscience to Refine Your Mind

Some people find it hard to believe in the soul, but its existence is the only possible explanation for some of my own and other people's experiences. If there is no such thing as a soul, how can we explain, for example, near-death experiences, wherein a person who "dies" from an illness or an accident finds herself floating above her body or catches glimpses of another mysterious world and then returns to life? A friend of mine lived through this very experience.

After collapsing from a heart attack, my friend was rushed to the hospital. Although his heart had stopped beating, the medical team eventually managed to bring him back to life. He later told me, however, that as he lingered between life and death, he found himself walking in a field full of flowers. For some reason, he saw me coming toward him. I approached him in the field and asked, "What are you doing here?" at which point he suddenly came to his senses and found that he was lying in bed.

My friend's near-death experience impressed upon me the fact that our bodies and our souls are separate entities. His description of the world he saw while his body lay dying was vivid and real, and he was so completely in this other world that he could remember the experience in detail. I understood my friend's experience to mean that our souls must be in a different "place" than our bodies.

According to the Buddhist concept of the transmigration of the soul, when we are born into this world, our souls carry with them the karma that we have accumulated from previous lives, and before we die, we will add our experiences from this life to our eternal storehouse of karma. Hidden beneath our many tiers of karma are our true selves, our eternal souls that have the pure, beautiful nature of the Buddha. If we could become the embodiment of our true selves, we would be Buddha-like, pure-hearted and with pure thoughts, capable only of good deeds. It is our karma-cloaked souls, our desire-filled instincts, and the like, that veil the true self and prevent its manifestation.

We can use practices such as zazen and yoga to help us refine our minds. In the same manner that we would polish a lens, these practices work from the outside in, removing one barrier after another, rubbing the intellect down to the layer of sensation, polishing through sensations and emotions to instinct and then continuing to buff until the true self is exposed. When we work to thoroughly refine our minds, we are engaging in religious practice, and we will reach the state of enlightenment only when we have rubbed away the dross until all that remains is the true self.

119

When we achieve enlightenment, we understand all truths and gain the *chie* of the Buddha. Those who are enlightened are no longer captive to their instincts or senses and are able to dedicate themselves solely to serving others and society. But for ordinary people, it's impossible to reach the state of enlightenment. What, then, should we do?

I think that ordinary people must strive to suppress and control our instincts and sensations with our intelligence and conscience. We must obey our intelligence and conscience, both of which originate in the true self and the soul, and imprint unshakable ethical and moral guidelines in our minds. We must engrave on our minds a spirit of dedicated service to others and embrace contentment, the virtue through which we gain freedom from greed and worldly desire.

As we walk through life and accumulate "good experience," we can refine our minds and draw closer to enlightenment by learning to control our sensations and instincts with our intelligence and conscience. If we elevate our souls in this manner, we will continue on into the next world.

Even the Smallest Thing Has a Role

What is the essence of a human being? Why were we born? We must pursue these questions as long as we live. Toshihiko Izutsu (1914–1993), a scholar of Islam and Asian philosophy, offered what he thought it means to be a human being.

When we meditate to gain an understanding of the essence of a human being, we approach a state of consciousness that is exquisite, pure, and infinitely transparent. Our awareness of our existence grows acute at the same time that our awareness of our physical senses disappears. As we sink deeper and deeper into meditation, we enter a state of consciousness that can only be described as being, at which point in time we become aware that all creation is composed of that which can only be described as being. It is the attainment of this state of awareness that represents the essence of a human being.

The director of the Agency for Cultural Affairs, a psychologist named Hayao Kawai (1928–2007), joked that Izutsu's explanation of the essence of being made him want to say, "You there, flower, I see you're playing the role of a flower. My being is playing the part of Hayao Kawai." Usually, when we see a flower, we think, "There is a flower," but instead, Kawai was saying, "This being here is *acting* as a flower."

If we remove all the attributes that constitute a living creature— the body, the spirit, awareness, and the senses—all that remains is an essence that can only be called being. The core essence of being is common to all creation and resides within not just humans but all living things. At times being may take the form of a flower, and at other times the form of a human. In other words, the man named Kazuo Inamori did not exist originally. Rather, some being happened to take the physical form of my body. Likewise, the founder of Kyocera or KDDI didn't have to be me. I just happen to be performing those particular roles, which heaven bestowed upon me.

Heaven gives every person a role to play, and each of us spends our lives playing our particular role. In that sense, the weight or value of each person's existence is the same. As I explained in Chapter 2, everything in existence, from human beings and living creatures to each tree or blade of grass or even a pebble on the street, has been given a job to do by the Creator. All exist in accordance with the will of the universe.

Governing the universe is the law of conservation of energy, which states that while the total amount of energy in existence is fixed, energy has the capacity to change forms. For example, if you chop down a tree, turn it into firewood, and burn it, the

121

original energy of the tree has been turned into thermal energy and vapor. The sum total of the tree's energy has not changed, although its form has been modified. If we are to believe the law of conservation of energy, even a single pebble is indispensable to the formation of the universe. Everything, no matter how small, is essential to the existence of the universe.

Striving to Live the Ideal Leads to a Bright Future

All in existence forms a part of an enormous living entity—the universe. Not one creature, plant, or pebble came into being by chance. Every single bit of matter, no matter if it is organic or inorganic, exists because it is essential to the continuation of the universe.

I believe that humankind was created to fulfill a greater mission than any other living being. Humans were born on this planet with intellect and reason, with minds and souls filled with love and compassion. The universe has given human beings the extremely important responsibility to lord over creation, and we are therefore obligated to both recognize our unique universal role and strive diligently to refine our souls during our lifetimes. We must exercise diligence at all times so that our souls may be that much more beautiful than they were when we were born. The beautification and refinement of our souls, after all, is one of the reasons for our temporal existence.

Our lives take on their true meanings when we do our best at the ordinary things in life: working hard, being thankful, thinking good thoughts, doing the right thing, practicing self-reflection and self-discipline, refining our minds, and elevating our character in everyday life. Humankind should approach life in no other way than with this spirit of diligence. In the chaos of today's world, people are struggling to find their way through the dark night, yet I cannot help envisioning a brilliant future filled with hope. I long with all my heart for the realization of a world in which everyone can live fruitful, happy, fulfilling lives, and I am convinced that we can achieve such an existence.

If we practice the approach to life that I have proposed in this book, every individual, family, business, and nation will progress in a positive direction and achieve great results. A better tomorrow will come when each individual understands the noble mission with which he or she has been entrusted and strives to live in a way that is right as a human being. I am convinced that this way of life will lead to a radiant dawn for all.

Afterword

The title of this book, *A Compass to Fulfillment*, applies not only to the lives of individuals but also to those of companies, nations, civilizations, and the entire human race. Each one of these entities is an aggregate of individuals and therefore it too must follow the ideal way of living.

During my youth, when I strove to live as a better human being despite my many setbacks; later, during my years as a business manager, when I sought to discern the principles that would lead to success and prosperity for human beings; and now, when I have left the front lines of the business world and am contemplating the meaning of life through faith, I have confronted life honestly and gradually built up a way of living. In this book I have done my best to convey as frankly as possible what that way of life is.

As I conclude the writing of this book, I am filled with contentment, perhaps because *A Compass to Fulfillment* gave me the opportunity to express my thoughts fully and completely. It is my sincere hope that this book will serve as a compass for those who are searching earnestly for a way to live their lives in a chaotic world.

In closing, I would like to express my sincere appreciation to Nobutaka Ueki, president of Sunmark Publishing Inc., and to my editor, Ryuya Saito, for their dedicated efforts that made publication of this book possible. I would also like to thank Yoshihito Ota, general manager of the Kyocera corporate office of the chief executives, and Masashi Kasuya from Kyocera's management research department, for their invaluable support, as well as the many other people involved in publishing this book.

INDEX

ABOUT THE AUTHOR

Dr. Kazuo Inamori, whose management philosophy is shared in this book, is the founder and chairman of both Kyocera and DDI Corporation. He has been named Japan's most outstanding entrepreneur on multiple occasions.

Dr. Inamori was born on January 30, 1932, the second son of a struggling family with seven children, and grew up in the southern prefecture of Kagoshima. At age 27, he and seven colleagues founded Kyoto Ceramic Co. Ltd. with the equivalent of $10,000 in borrowed money. Known today as Kyocera Corporation, the company appears on both the Fortune 500 (#373 with annual sales of about $4 billion) and the *BusinessWeek* Global 1000 (#179 with market valuation of $12 billion).

In 1971, Kyocera became the first Japanese company to establish manufacturing operations in California. Its shares have been traded on the New York Stock Exchange since 1980, and four Americans now sit on its board.

In 1984, Dr. Inamori led 225 other companies in the formation of DDI Corporation, the first and largest privatized telephone company to challenge the monopoly of Nippon Telegraph and Telephone (NTT). As its chairman, Dr. Inamori directed DDI to form and operate eight regional cellular telephone subsidiaries in Japan.

In 1993, Kyocera and DDI formed Nippon Iridium. Today, Motorola and Nippon Iridium are the two largest investors in the Iridium Project—a global satellite network that will permit telephone communication between any two points on earth. DDI generated a profit of a half-billion dollars on sales of almost $4 billion and went public the same year.

In 1995, DDI advanced into the emerging personal communications system arena with nine subsidiaries that offer "pocket" telephone service in every major Japanese city.

Dr. Inamori's personal donation of $200 million in 1984 established the Inamori Foundation and its annual Kyoto Prizes as a way of repaying society for his success. Each year, three prizes representing the categories of Basic Science, Advanced Technology, and Creative Arts and Moral Sciences are awarded to outstanding individuals or group along with cash awards of approximately $500,000 each. As of the foundation's tenth anniversary, these prizes have been awarded to 2 Japanese, 16 Europeans, and 13 Americans.

CPSIA information can be obtained
at www.ICGtesting.com
Printed in the USA
JSHW042017110622
26518JS00004B/38